GETTING THROUGH THE

TOUGH
STUFF

GETTING THROUGH THE

TOUGH STUFF

It's Always Something!

CHARLES R. SWINDOLL

W PUBLISHING GROUP

A Division of Thomas Nelson Publishers

Since 1798

www.wpublishinggroup.com

GETTING THROUGH THE TOUGH STUFF

Charles R. Swindoll

Published by the W Publishing Group, a division of Thomas Nelson Inc., P. O. Box 141000, Nashville, Tennessee 37214.

W Publishing Group books may be puchased in bulk for educational, business, fundraising, or sales promotional use. For information, please email specialmarkets@ThomasNelson.com.

Unless otherwise noted, Scriptures are from the New American Standard Bible © 1960, 1962, 1968, 1971, 1972, 1973, 1975, 1977, 1995 by The Lockman Foundation. Used by permission.

Scriptures noted as MSG are quoted from The Message, copyright © 1993, 1994, 1995, 1996 by Eugene H. Peterson. Used by permission of NavPress Publishing Group.

Library of Congress Cataloging-in-Publication Data

Swindoll, Charles R.
   Getting through the tough stuff : it's always something! / Charles R. Swindoll
   p. cm.
   Includes bibliographical references.

ISBN 0-8499-1813-8

1. Life cycle, Human—Religious aspects—Christianity.   2. Consolation.
3. Christian life.   I. Title.
BV4597.555.S95   2004
                                                    CIP

Printed in the United States of America
04 05 06 07 08 QWP 5 4 3 2 1

It is with great gratitude for her life

and her remarkable responses to

the tough stuff of life

that I dedicate this volume to

our older daughter,

CHARISSA ANN SWINDOLL.

Her mother and I give God

maximum praise for sustaining her

"through many dangers, toils, and snares."

It was grace that brought her safe thus far,

and it will be grace that will enable her

to encourage others to press on

for the rest of her years on earth.

Contents

CONTENTS

Introduction

Life is like an onion, which one peels crying. —FRENCH PROVERB

When you are down and out, something always turns up—and it's usually the noses of your friends. —ORSON WELLES

Life's a tough proposition, and the first hundred years are the hardest.
—WILSON MIZNER

LIFE AND TOUGH STUFF GO HAND IN HAND. They typically appear as gradually intensifying storms. Sometimes sudden winds of adversity hit hard against us as our barometers take a dive to the bottom of the gauge.

Maybe you're there right now. That's why you chose this book. Tough stuff seems easier to manage when we see it coming. But how often does that happen? It's the treacherous assaults beyond the horizon, those mental muggings we cannot see, that buckle our knees. You know exactly what I mean.

Adversity has a way of cutting us down. After the initial blunt blow, we're left stunned, wondering what hit us. It's the tough stuff that tests the core of our beings, leaving us with contrasting results. It will either strengthen our deepest beliefs or unravel the fabric of our faith. Everything depends on our response. Occasionally the blows are so brutal they alter life as we know it.

I read of a couple who worked long and hard on the East Coast to put away a down payment for a home. They labored for years to save money, planned wisely, and managed precious funds with great thrift and care. Finally they achieved their goal and made plans to purchase their first home. It was the summer of 1989. Their hearts were set on a lovely little home just outside Charleston. The paperwork was in order. The house was ready. The dream would soon be reality. But on the morning of September 22, Hurricane Hugo slammed onto the eastern seaboard, wreaking mind-boggling destruction. As you may recall, Charleston took a direct hit. Without warning, the couple's new home, representing their cherished dreams for the future, was washed away in Hugo's monstrous surge. When the water receded, only a soggy pile of nightmares and some painfully difficult decisions lay before them. Tough stuff to get through.

If you can't identify with that, maybe with this example you can. You haven't had a physical for two or three years and you decide to visit your physician for a thorough exam. She spends a day or more testing, poking, scanning, and listening. She doesn't say much, but within a few hours after you've returned home, your phone rings. The doctor asks you to come back for a follow-up consultation. In her office she mentions that a troublesome sign showed up on one of the tests. She can't say for sure what it means. The following day, after the scans are studied, she confirms the presence of a tumor.

Surgery follows. It doesn't look good. A few more agonizingly uncertain days drag by, and finally you hear the dread report: *cancer.* It's an aggressive form that leaves little hope for survival past a year, if that. That's tough stuff in spades.

Let's say you've been married for thirty years. You remember with mixed emotions your thirtieth anniversary five months ago . . . those two weeks you spent alone on Maui. Though the weather was perfect, with those prevailing ocean winds blowing across the beach, your husband stayed quiet and sullen. You let it pass, not wanting to spoil an idyllic anniversary vacation. A few weeks later he sits down and with an expressionless gaze utters, "There's someone else in my life. I just don't love you anymore." The shock leaves you numb. Your head spins. You've watched other couples struggle through a devastating breakup, but you never dreamed it would one day be you. Yet you're right there, right now, trying to get through your most difficult and disillusioned days, at the time in life when years are meant to be enjoyed, not endured. The children are raised and retirement is near. No longer. Not now. Today you face a future, alone. You're preoccupied with haunted thoughts of financial ruin mixed with confusing days of wondering what went wrong. Really tough stuff.

Here's one more. You're one of those brave patriotic mothers or fathers who watched proudly as your now-grown son boarded a military transport in full combat gear, bound for some spot in the Middle East you can't even pronounce. You've supported him in his decision to join the Marines, train hard, and now launch out into his first overseas deployment. The conflict in that war-torn region has never cooled to less than a simmer. Now it has heated to a boil, and your only son will step off that aircraft in the thick of it. You wait anxiously for word of his safe arrival. Instead, scattered news bulletins begin delivering sketchy details of a downed helicopter somewhere in the desert. What are the odds? Surely he's safe. God wouldn't let him be taken! But a call from a somber-voiced chaplain confirms your worst fears. Tears run down your face as reality eclipses hope. Your son is dead, killed with six others in an unexplained crash.

Nothing can prepare you for such devastating circumstances. Life is a coat that never fits right. We are forever cinching up here, taking in there, letting out over here. Life doesn't fit our plans. We exist in a continual state of maneuvering, adjusting, shifting, believing, often doubting. Getting through the tough stuff requires it.

Thankfully God has provided us with the right perspective. He has made available a Savior, and His name is Jesus. He wants to take the blows for you, to help you through the tough stuff. Truth be told, He can become the rudder of your life when fierce winds blow, your reliable compass when you've lost your bearings, your harbor when sailing on isn't possible. He's the answer. He intersects you at life's most critical crossroads and makes all the difference.

In the chapters that follow I want to lead you on a walk through a random selection of the first four books of the New Testament. We will visit various scenes from Jesus's life and ministry—those places where He faced His own tough stuff and met others who were experiencing the same. We'll discover how He not only met them but how He reached out, offering a helping hand to lead them through. Because He remains "the same yesterday, today, and forever," no storm is too devastating, no climb is too steep. He can handle it. He can get you through. As a matter of fact He can empower you with supernatural strength in the process.

There's an old translation of the New Testament by Charles B. Williams, titled *The New Testament in the Language of the People*. In that excellent translation a footnote at Philippians 4:13 reads, "I have power for all things through Him who puts a dynamo in me."[1]

Isn't that great? When Christ comes into your life, He places a *dynamo* there. It's a power pack that can be adjusted and adapted, tightening up when necessary or letting out slack. It can release or hold back, depending on the terrain. It can control. It can keep things on a fairly tranquil plane. How? Why? Because *He* is present. That's the ticket—His presence hard at work deep within your being.

More on that later.

Before we proceed, allow me a few lines to acknowledge some folks who have helped to make this book a reality. My longtime friend and very gifted editor in Chicago, Mark Tobey, invested hundreds of hours as he transformed my words into meaningful expressions. Once again Carol Spencer, here in Frisco, Texas, provided her able assistance as she researched the footnotes and secured all the rights and permissions. Finally, Mary Hollingsworth at Shady Oaks Studio in Fort Worth and her splendid team of editors, readers, and typesetters gave the book its shape and format, which meant the final touches were carefully and professionally brought to completion. My heartfelt thanks to all!

Now it's time to get started. Whether you've been hit broadside by an unforeseen blast or you're watching ominous clouds approach in the distance, you probably need somebody to help you get through the tough stuff.

I'm ready if you are. You have nothing to fear. You really don't. There's help available from the God who loves you. Just turn the page where we'll discover it together.

—CHARLES SWINDOLL

One

Getting Through the Tough Stuff of Temptation

A FAVORITE POEM OF MINE is Robert Frost's "The Road Not Taken." It speaks plainly of the importance of going the right way when tempted to take another.

> Two roads diverged in a yellow wood,
> And sorry I could not travel both
> And be one traveler, long I stood
> And looked down one as far as I could
> To where it bent in the undergrowth;
>
> Then took the other, as just as fair,
> And having perhaps the better claim,
> Because it was grassy and wanted wear;
> Though as for that, the passing there

Had worn them really about the same,
And both that morning equally lay
In leaves no step had trodden black.
Oh, I kept the first for another day!
Yet knowing how way leads on to way,
I doubted if I should ever come back.

I shall be telling this with a sigh
Somewhere ages and ages hence:
Two roads diverged in a wood, and I—
I took the one less traveled by,
And that has made all the difference.[1]

Temptations come like Frost's proverbial fork in the road. We determine our destiny in how we respond. Take the wrong road and the end could be devastating. That's what makes our struggle with temptations so unbelievably tough. It's those consequences we don't want to face that haunt us.

But before we address our struggle, let's look at the temptation Jesus faced. Our journey begins with a critical juncture in His life. That scene is described near the beginning of the Gospel story written by Matthew. It's important you read the entire account to grasp the nature of this diabolical ordeal. Let its intensity grip you.

Then Jesus was led up by the Spirit into the wilderness to be tempted by the devil. And after He had fasted forty days and forty nights, He then became hungry. And the tempter came and said to Him, "If You are the Son of God, command that these stones become bread." But He answered and said, "It is written, 'MAN SHALL NOT LIVE ON BREAD ALONE, BUT ON EVERY WORD THAT PROCEEDS OUT OF THE MOUTH OF GOD.'"

Then the devil took Him into the holy city and had Him stand on the pinnacle of the temple, and said to Him, "If You are the Son of God, throw Yourself down, for it is written,

'HE WILL COMMAND HIS ANGELS CONCERNING YOU'; and 'ON THEIR HANDS THEY WILL BEAR YOU UP, SO THAT YOU WILL NOT STRIKE YOUR FOOT AGAINST A STONE.'"

Jesus said to him, "On the other hand, it is written, 'YOU SHALL NOT PUT THE LORD YOUR GOD TO THE TEST.'"

Again, the devil took Him to a very high mountain and showed Him all the kingdoms of the world and their glory; and he said to Him, "All these things I will give You, if You fall down and worship me." Then Jesus said to him, "Go, Satan! For it is written, 'YOU SHALL WORSHIP THE LORD YOUR GOD, AND SERVE HIM ONLY.'" Then the devil left Him; and behold, angels came and began to minister to Him. (Matthew 4:1–11)

WHEN JESUS MEETS THE TEMPTER

Matthew 4 opens at the commencement of Jesus's ministry. His official work had not yet begun. He was a thirty-year-old single adult. He had not yet called the twelve disciples. He hadn't delivered His first sermon. He had not even been criticized. He was young, inexperienced, and virtually unknown.

At His baptism in the chilly Jordan River, Jesus's message and mission were verified as God announced, "This is My beloved Son, in whom I am well-pleased" (Matthew 3:17). And with that the Spirit immediately whisked Jesus away to an unnamed wilderness. Alone and pensive, Jesus fasted for forty days and nights. When He lay weakened from lack of nourishment and languishing in the harsh desert elements, the tempter made his move.

Isn't that a clever strategy? The enemy knows exactly when you and I are most vulnerable. He knows to look patiently for that chink in our armor where we're most exposed. Satan waited until Christ seemed most vulnerable before he initiated a series of three grueling tests. Each became more intense than the one before.

THE NATURE OF THE TEMPTATIONS

In the first temptation the devil taunted Jesus, who answered him with Scripture. Instead of backing off, Satan taunted Jesus a second time. Again Jesus met his adversary's test with the power of biblical truth. Undeterred, Satan persisted. He escorted Jesus to an exceedingly high mountain, tempting Him for the third time. Jesus's answer was a leveling reply, which came again with the force of Scripture. Back and forth it went. We call it *interchange,* a rhetorical device Matthew employed to make his point. Matthew wanted his readers to catch the force of Satan's relentless, repeated assaults, each of which was met by Christ's firm resistance.

Remember, Jesus didn't come as a conquering, warrior King storming the world with fireworks, flags, and fanfare. That's how you and I would come if we wanted to be king! Not Jesus. Matthew explains how Christ came as a lowly King to inaugurate a different kind of kingdom. He came silently and humbly, like a soft-footed servant, slipping into the darkness of earth's night without anyone noticing. He entered without pretense but not without purpose. He came to die . . . to pay sin's penalty in full. His mission was the Cross, and nobody knew that more than Satan. The devil's strategy to thwart that mission was to take Jesus off point before His ministry even began. He hoped to trick God's Son into submission, using a three-pronged line of attack.

The first temptation was of a personal nature. The tempter slipped in and whispered in His ear, "If You are the Son of God, command that these stones become bread." At their feet were small, smooth stones, perhaps chips of limestone abundant in that wilderness terrain. Jesus had just completed forty days of fasting, and His body had grown weak and hungry. Satan tempts the starving young man to take matters into His own hands. How easy it would have been for Jesus to yield and attend to His personal needs. By now Jesus was abundantly aware of His superlative gifts and powers. He could have picked up a handful of those stones and instantly become the bread king. Given His compassion, He could have filled the stomachs of hungry children and emaciated families all across that region. What a dramatic way to win the hearts of the people to His cause! Who wouldn't follow such a miracle worker? That's why the enticement was *personal.* It was as if Satan was suggesting, "You could become Messiah without ever having to go to the cross!"

Jesus saw right through the devil's plot and replied, "It is written, 'Man shall not live on bread alone, but on every word that proceeds out of the mouth of God.'" What a magnificent answer! What a statement to make on an empty stomach! Jesus knew more was at stake than His physical needs. He came to redeem the human soul. Jesus resisted the temptation to use His gifts to parade His glory for selfish reasons. He came to do the Father's will and to fulfill His splendid purpose. So He wasted no time rejecting the temptation to abuse His power.

I'm convinced that most of us are rarely tempted in the area of our weaknesses but far more often in the areas of our strengths. I'm not the first to point that out. One man writes,

> We must always remember that again and again we are tempted through our gifts. The person who is gifted with charm will be

tempted to use that charm "to get away with anything." The person who is gifted with the power of words will be tempted to use his command of words to produce glib excuses to justify his own conduct. The person with a vivid and sensitive imagination will undergo agonies of temptation that a more stoic person will never experience. The person with great gifts of mind will be tempted to use these gifts for himself, and not for others, to become the master and not the servant of men. It is the grim fact of temptation that it is just where we are strongest that we must be forever on the watch.[2]

God has gifted each of us with inner abilities and giftedness—not to turn stones into food, but to turn words into pictures. Some enjoy remarkable gifts of persuasion. Unchecked, you easily give in to the temptation to sell out to lower aims than the noble purposes God has designed. Those gifted in the area of discipline can be tempted to take corrective measures too far, even to abusive extremes. Those are temptations of a personal nature that lure us into dangerous patterns of self-satisfaction.

In one of the toughest stretches of His life, Jesus resisted that personal temptation. But the devil persisted.

The second temptation was one of a public nature. Next, Satan took Jesus to the city of Jerusalem to a high place. If I've got this place located correctly, they were together at the uppermost point of the temple complex, four hundred and fifty feet above the base of the Kidron Valley. That's forty-five stories up! Standing there next to the King of kings, the devil snarled, "If You are the Son of God, throw Yourself down, for it is written, 'He will command His angels concerning You. . . . On their hands they will bear You up, so that You will not strike Your foot against a stone.'" Quoting from Psalm 91,

Satan presumptuously pressed for a public display of God's power to protect Jesus from certain death.

Imagine, Satan was tempting Jesus to make a swan dive off the pinnacle of Solomon's temple! Satan wanted sensationalism. The devil knew God would not allow His Son to die, at least not yet, not like that. His death would be a cruel, agonizing death at Calvary. He would not have died had He jumped. He would have been preserved. The devil might have said something like, "What an opportunity to make an impact! [No pun intended.] You'll have people from all over following You as a wonder worker, a sensationalist who can jump from the pinnacle and live to tell the story. Just imagine it. It would make the tabloids. Cable news! Think of the people who would believe in You! And You wouldn't have to hang on that rugged cross. What a deal! I mean, a little sensationalism never hurt anybody, Jesus. People love it!"

Again, Jesus saw straight through the devil's plan and delivered another diffusing response, saying, "You shall not put the Lord your God to the test."

Using Scripture as a shield, Jesus avoided committing what the Bible describes as the sin of presumption—presuming on God and His people. Only God knows how many religious workers dance on the edge of that temptation. What's wrong with a touch of sensationalism? Why not flirt with a little danger or live on the edge of reckless foolishness and claim deliverance by divine intervention? Why not do that, especially if it draws a crowd? What's wrong with that? Two reasons come to mind:

First, attracting people by sensationalism starts a process you can never complete. One sensationalistic act requires a second . . . and it needs to be greater than the first. And the second act requires one greater than that for the third. Soon you're trapped in a never-ending downward cycle. You have to keep doing one better than the last to keep the crowd coming.

Second, sensationalism draws attention to an individual rather than to the living God. It creates a circus atmosphere.

Really, though, what's wrong with a little snake handling if God protects? What's wrong with a leap into space every now and then if you need a crowd? I appreciate the caution in a statement I read recently: "A gospel founded on sensation-mongering is foredoomed to failure."[3] Sure, Jesus would have lived through the leap, but the temptation was to see if He would rely on a sensational trick rather than the power of the Cross. Thankfully in the tough stuff of satanic allurement Jesus resisted temptation of a public nature. As always, the tempter had one more test up his sleeve.

The third temptation was of a power nature. Jesus and Satan left the pinnacle of the temple and were quickly swept even farther up to the peak of a mountain overlooking the kingdoms of the known world. Who knows how high? Beyond each horizon stretched an expanse of lands and empires. We can only imagine the panoramic scene below. You and I have been in high places where we've looked out over a city of lights or across a sparkling lake. Those views left us breathless. But none of that compares to what the two of them, all alone, must of have seen.

God had plans for His Son to rule the kingdoms of the earth, but that plan did not include Satan's presumptuous offer. I repeat, the Father's plan would be fulfilled through the cross of suffering and only there. Satan loathed the thought of Jesus making it to Calvary. Lucifer knew the cross represented the place he'd experience his doom. The cross, therefore, was not an option for the devil. He tempted Jesus to gain that power by obeying and worshiping him, not Almighty God.

The Outcome of the Temptations

A few years ago, while traveling to a conference ground with my friend Chuck Colson, former confidant and White House chief of staff for President Richard Nixon, I asked why anyone would want to be president. To me, there isn't enough money or prestige in the world to make life worth the hassle and the effort. He smiled and answered rather quickly, "One word, my friend: POWER. It all comes down to power."[4] Few of us will ever be tempted to pursue presidential power. But we're tempted to maneuver our way to power through other schemes, aren't we? The devil knows we crave it. Is it any wonder that he baits us to go there?

When he does, Jesus's model is a good one to follow.

Without hesitation, He replied, "Go, Satan! For it is written, 'You shall worship the Lord your God, and serve Him only.'" If you've been looking for an illustration of "just say no," search no further. And with that, Matthew concludes, "the devil left Him."

Wouldn't it be great if the tough stuff of all our temptations came and left as quickly as that? Bam, bam, bam . . . one, two, three . . . and we're done. Unfortunately that's the exception, not the rule.

When the Tempter Comes Your Way

On one hand, today you may find yourself in a situation of relative peace and comfort. No real worries. Bills are up-to-date, portfolio looks impressive, kids are on track, job is secure. Check. Life is good. On the other hand, your life may have fallen on the rocks. Nothing is working out the way you planned. You can't seem to get the break you need. You've prayed your heart out for weeks, maybe months. No answer. Nothing. God has seemingly checked out. You're worn down and wondering if the sun will ever shine again. Whichever may be your situation, remain on guard. In comfort or distress, you're easy prey. If you listen closely, you will hear the hiss of the enemy's voice. Simply worship him, pick up the lifestyle he suggests, and you're home free. Before you know it, you've complicated things, and the tough stuff of temptation intensifies.

Temptation is not a crossroad only Jesus had to face. That's a common fork in the road. You will find yourself there before the week grinds to an end. Your experience won't come as dramatically as a personal visit from the devil, but another temptation will come. Then another. And another.

What am I suggesting? Clearly, you need to be ready. That's why I want to offer three simple yet effective strategies to help you resist the pull of temptation and not be caught unprepared.

First, don't be alarmed; expect it. You cannot be promoted in your career beyond the level of temptation. You cannot know a life so peaceful that you're finally so secure you're protected from Satan's assaults. Temptations begin as inner battles fought in the mind and as unseen struggles of the will. They attack you in the deep recesses of your heart. Interestingly, nobody knows. Expecting temptation helps keep you alert for the spiritual battle. When Paul wrote to the Corinthian Christians, he encouraged them to keep short accounts with one another in order that "no advantage would be taken of us by Satan, for we are not ignorant of his schemes" (2 Corinthians 2:11).

Let me get painfully specific here. A major, hidden battleground of temptation today is Internet pornography. The statistics of those who are addicted is staggering, not to mention those who turn to it in the secrecy of their undetected worlds. Knowing how pervasive and insidious this temptation really is requires me to stay alert and ready. Every month thousands of new porn sites appear on the

Internet. And many of them are tucked away, ready to fill your screen even when you're not seeking them.

While trying to find a map to a little town in north Texas where several friends and I could ride our Harleys and then eat a barbeque lunch together, I punched in the name of that town. That's it—that's all I entered into my computer. Immediately, in bold, one-inch letters, I saw "SEX" on my screen. And that was only the beginning. As I tried to remove it, each new attempt brought up more lurid scenes. Not even when I punched Escape was I able to escape the recurring scenes, each one intensely alluring to the flesh.

Determined, I reached down and turned my computer off . . . completely off. Finally! But would you believe? When I later turned it on, there it was again—another unwanted but very real temptation. Thankfully, my younger son, Chuck, was able to find a way to free the equipment. And it all started while on a simple, rather hurried search for a little town in north Texas. Being alert to this reality is essential.

This is a good time for me to mention a couple of excellent electronic tools to help all who use a computer. BsafeOnline and NetAccountability make the best use of technology and Christian relationships to defeat the adversary. BsafeOnline's web filterlink software effectively blocks Internet porn before it enters your home or office. NetAccountability software is an online "buddy system" that adds teeth to real life accountability. For a small fee, you can use their program to help fight this temptation. You select a partner of your choice with whom you enter into an accountability relationship. He or she is given access to your Internet activity and you, in turn, are allowed access to your partner's activity. That way, at any time, you or your partner can quickly scan what the other has been watching. Knowing that your partner is holding you accountable is a deterrent that helps you resist the temptation.

Check out www.netaccountability.com for yourself. I've personally found it extremely effective, and therefore I recommend it often
and enthusiastically. You might also visit the Insight for Living Web
site at www.insight.org for links to Bible study tools and other helpful Web sites that can help protect your home and office from the
tempting grip of pornography.

These are good ways to stay alert to the tempter. Don't be
alarmed by temptation; expect it.

Second, don't be blind; detect it. Call temptation what it is. Because
the adversary has innumerable methods of attack, and because they
are seldom overt, we're often blindsided by him. We need to ask God
to help us detect his presence and brace ourselves for the impact.

An ink-stained wall in the Wartburg Castle in Germany illustrates my point. It's part of a room once occupied by the great
reformer Martin Luther, who in the midst of prayer and study
detected the presence of the enemy. The story goes that he picked up
his inkpot and hurled it against the wall as he aimed at the devil.
Luther sensed the adversary's sinister advance and responded the
best he way knew how.

Do you have that kind of spiritual sensitivity? Cynthia and I have
been in places where we've both sensed the palpable presence of evil.
Believe me, we're not the witch-hunting types. We're not the kind of
folks who see demons in every dark alley or behind every door.
That's not us. But we stay extremely sensitive to evil's realities. On
occasion one of us will whisper in the other's ear, "The enemy is in
this. It's not of the Lord. Let's get out!"

A spiritually sensitive spouse is a magnificent gift from the
Lord. But if you don't have that, seek out a friend who understands
the tough stuff you wrestle with and the intensity of your struggle.
The support will be invaluable. A trusted friend can help keep you

in check, support you in prayer, and be there when you begin to weaken. Alcoholics Anonymous has operated on this basis for years. When you start to falter, someone willing to assist and strengthen you is only a phone call away.

Believe me, inkpots cannot frustrate the devil permanently. Temptation will come again. So, don't be blind; detect it.

Third, don't be clever; reject it. I find less mature believers naively think they can sort of roll up their spiritual sleeves and challenge the devil to a duel. What a foolish thought! Try that approach and you will lose every time. Attempt to play clever games with the enemy and he'll pick you clean. Don't even go near there. Instead, do what the apostle James commands: "Submit therefore to God. Resist the devil and he will flee from you" (James 4:7). The key word is *resist*. Wonderful advice. And notice that exhortation comes in two steps: Submit to God. Resist the devil. Satan would have you reverse the command and do the opposite. He wants you to resist God and submit to him. That's a trap! Don't be clever; reject it.

A FINAL WORD OF HOPE

Tucked away in Hebrews 4 are some extremely comforting words for those who are determined to get through the tough stuff of temptation. Read this section of Holy Scripture slowly and carefully. I really don't want you to miss the power and hope these verses contain.

> For we do not have a high priest who cannot sympathize with our weaknesses, but One who has been tempted in all things as we are, yet without sin. Therefore let us draw near with confidence to the throne of grace, so that we may receive mercy and find grace to help in time of need. (Hebrews 4:15–16)

For the longest time I struggled to understand the meaning of those words. What I couldn't grasp was *how* Jesus could have been tempted in all the ways I have been tempted. Think through the logic. First, I've lived longer than Jesus lived. Many who read this book have no doubt lived longer than I. Jesus lived only thirty-three years and then He was gone. Only three of those thirty-three years were spent in public ministry. So how, for example, could He have known the temptations that come with aging? Or how would He possibly understand the temptations of a young soldier stationed in England during World War II? How could He relate to the intense struggles of a young, professional woman trying to achieve success in twenty-first-century America? We're missing something if that's our logic.

Christ didn't experience every single temptation that you or I have faced. That's not what this means. But He did absorb the full brunt of the enemy's power and endured it without yielding to sin. No other human being could withstand the unbridled force of Satan's power. Some Christians may handle 30 percent of the enemy's power. Some may have faith strong enough to take 50 percent of his attack before they yield. Some perhaps 70 percent. Yet no one, except Jesus Christ Himself, has withstood the all-out force—100 percent of Satan's fury. Christ, our High Priest, endured it all for you. That's why He's such a reliable resource to get you through the tough stuff of temptation. He's been there. He's felt that sting. And He strengthens us with power to stand firm.

I appreciate the way Eugene Peterson paraphrases this in *The Message:*

> We don't have a priest who is out of touch with our reality. He's
> been through weakness and testing, experienced it all—all but

the sin. So let's walk right up to him and get what he is so ready
to give. Take the mercy, accept the help.

That's why leaning on and trusting in Christ during the tough
stuff of life makes so much sense. No other person but Jesus Christ
could say, "I have gone all the way through the attacks of the enemy.
And when you face your own temptations, you can rely on Me. I
have the power, I can provide the dynamo you need to endure. Take
the mercy; accept the help."

Thankfully, your options are down to one. What you need is
Him. He's all you need! He is sufficient. By the way, Martin Luther
did more than just sling ink onto a castle wall. He used that ink to
write his magnificent hymn "A Mighty Fortress Is Our God." One
of those stanzas is too relevant to ignore.

> Did we in our own strength confide,
> Our striving would be losing,
> Were not the right man on our side,
> The man of God's own choosing.
> Dost ask who that may be?
> Christ Jesus, it is He—
> Lord Sabaoth His name,
> From age to age the same,
> And He must win the battle. [5]

If there is anyone who is qualified to win the battle, it is Jesus.
When you let Him fight it for you, He will. The question is a simple
one: *will you let Him?*

Two

Getting Through the Tough Stuff of Misunderstanding

"To be great is to be misunderstood," said Ralph Waldo Emerson.[1] As you read that you may think, *If that's true, I'm greater than I thought!* Few things in life are harder to endure than being misunderstood. To make matters worse, being misunderstood is such a common human experience. We can be cruising along fairly well when suddenly we collide head-on with someone who misunderstands our actions or misjudges our motives. As a result, we can spend months, sometimes years, expending precious energy trying to climb out of the wreckage. The tough stuff of misunderstanding reminds me of hockey.

Hockey players love head-on collisions. Could that be why the game was invented? Two teams of six players on ice skates try to make a goal by smashing a three-inch rubber puck into the opponent's net. That's the easy part. What it turns out to be, though, is a game of nonstop, sanctioned collisions for athletes who love slamming into one another.

Sure, there's skill involved in playing hockey (I keep telling myself). I detect even a certain gracefulness about two strong men colliding on ice skates. But things can get ugly fast, especially when the gloves come flying off and the bloodletting begins. That's when you run for cover . . . unless you're a fan! Fans love those brawls. Soon both team benches have emptied as players stream onto the ice like killer bees and converge into an angry blur of numbers. The fists of number 47 are pounding 3's nose, who's tearing 50's jersey, who's kicking 13 in the gut, who's choking 65, who is jerking 74's face off along with his mask. About the only thing hockey players don't do to each other is bite, but that's because none of them have enough teeth left.

But real misunderstanding is no game. Life can get extremely ugly. Gloves fly off, emotions heat to a boil, and the result is a blur of chaos and pain. Getting through the tough stuff of misunderstanding can be a long and grueling ordeal. As we learned about facing temptations, we need to remember we're not alone.

MISUNDERSTOOD? YOU ARE NOT ALONE

Let me give you some examples from everyday life and then from the Bible. Both categories illustrate how these harsh collisions occur. Hopefully, you'll find comfort and help as you realize you're not the only person to face the struggle.

Some Everyday Examples

Let's imagine that you really want to assist someone in need. You take the risk of reaching out with compassion. Your motive is pure. Your heart is right. To your surprise, everything goes downhill from there.

Some jealous critic decides you're in it for yourself and starts questioning your motives. Nothing you say or do can change the critic's mind. You're now viewed as nosy and pushy, and you're verbally portrayed as one of those holier-than-thou, busybody Christians. Misunderstood.

Or you find out your friend is caught in a no-win situation. Part of the problem is her own doing. So you begin to pray. Again, your heart is right. After a while you begin to feel the Lord would have you lovingly confront her with the hope that she will be encouraged to take responsibility and change. No way! She explodes in your face questioning your *real* intentions. She sees you as judgmental. A once-warm friendship winds up on ice. Misunderstood.

In your zeal to help your company's year-end performance, you have a great idea. All on your own you turn things up a notch and bring a major product line in ahead of the market. It works beautifully. The result is a nice promotion and public recognition from the head of your division. Everybody applauds your creativity and diligence. Well, almost everybody. To your amazement, your direct supervisor thinks you're after his job. Threatened by your success, he begins to see you as too ambitious, presumptuous, and overconfident. He makes life miserable for you in the office. It turns into a big mess . . . all because you had a great idea and were trying to excel in your work. Misunderstood.

Thankfully, God didn't leave experiences in misunderstanding out of His Word. Tucked into the folds of Scripture are numerous examples of how even the Lord's choice servants felt the sting and were forced to endure the tough stuff of misunderstanding.

Two Examples from the Bible

After a few hurtful blows, life turned the corner for Joseph. He had been rejected and sold into slavery by his brothers. When the dust finally settled, he found himself in the house of Potiphar, a high-ranking official in Egypt. I should explain that those ornery brothers had misunderstood Joseph's special treatment by their father Jacob, which prompted them to rid themselves of Joseph once and for all. But the Scriptures say, "The Lord was with Joseph, so he became a successful man." Isn't that great? It only gets better. Read carefully how the story unfolds.

> Now his master saw that the LORD was with him and how the LORD caused all that he did to prosper in his hand. So Joseph found favor in his sight, and became his personal servant; and he made him overseer over his house, and all that he owned he put in his charge. It came about that from the time he made him overseer in his house and over all that he owned, the LORD blessed the Egyptian's house because of Joseph; thus the LORD's blessing was upon all that he owned, in the house and in the field. So he left everything he owned in Joseph's charge; and with him there he did not concern himself with anything except the food which he ate. Now Joseph was handsome in form and appearance. (Genesis 39:3–6)

Everything would have been ideal for the young man if it were not for that last minor detail: "Joseph was handsome in form and appearance." And Potiphar's wife wanted him for herself. Many times Joseph had rejected her seductive enticements. She refused to give up. The story goes that one day, as Joseph was going about his duties in the house, Potiphar's aggressive wife grabbed him in a lustful embrace. Joseph stood his ground. He freed himself then turned tail and split. Infuriated, she grabbed his cloak as he fled the room. She kept it as evidence to substantiate her accusation: "Rape! He tried to rape me!" Her baseless rant landed Joseph in an Egyptian dungeon, where he was forced to spend years in virtual obscurity. There was no explaining his way out of that one. He had been unjustly accused. The word is *misunderstood.*

Then there was David. The young shepherd spent his early years tending his father's sheep in the field. One day he heard his dad's whistle from the house. There stood Samuel, a prophet of the Lord who had come to anoint him with oil—oil fit for a king. King of Israel to be precise. One day David's tending sheep, the next he's told he will someday rule the nation. Not much changed after that, until one day David's father, Jesse, commissioned him to deliver a care package of food to his brothers, who were serving as soldiers with the army of Israel in a standoff with the Philistines. While visiting the battlefield on that errand, David noticed a giant rambling back and forth taunting the armies of Israel. He grew more indignant with each vile slur that poured from the giant's mouth. With one well-aimed fling of David's slingshot, the great enemy of Israel came crashing to the ground in the Valley of Elah. King Saul witnessed the entire event in drop-jaw amazement and then summoned David to his side. Invited into Saul's private court, David became the king's personal musician and servant. As it turns out, that was a little too close for comfort as envious Saul observed young David growing in the Lord's favor and with the people of Israel. He couldn't take it. It wasn't long before David's popularity enraged Saul, whose jealousy became so intense that he attempted to spear David. David spent the next twelve years living as a fugitive in the Judean wilderness. Another classic case of being misunderstood. Collisions with misunderstanding can derail the best of us.

Those Old Testament examples cause me to remember another who endured the tough stuff of misunderstanding. In fact, everything in His earthly existence from womb to tomb was wrapped in a tangled web of misunderstanding. His undeserved pain and suffering didn't simply *feel* like it lasted a lifetime, it did.

MISUNDERSTOOD? MEET THE ONE WHO UNDERSTANDS

The most misunderstood individual who ever lived was Jesus Christ. Critics joked about the circumstances of His birth. They disputed His divine origin with ethnic jeering and vicious taunts, even to the point of accusing Him of belonging to Satan. They scorned His purposes. They reviled His teachings. They were suspicious of His motives, critical of His methods, and angered by His message. Ultimately, the Jewish leaders conspired with the Roman officials to put Him to death. That explains what the apostle John meant when he wrote, "The Light shines in the darkness, and the darkness did not comprehend it. . . . He came to His own, and those who were His own did not receive Him" (John 1:5, 11). Christ came into an uncomprehending darkness where He met nothing but unbending misunderstanding.

Misunderstood by the Pharisees

Jesus inaugurated His ministry and authenticated His claims to be Messiah by performing miracles throughout the land. But it was those supernatural deeds that brought scorn and ridicule from the Pharisees, the religious leaders of Israel who misunderstood His redemptive mission.

The opening verses of Mark 3 set the stage for the initial conflict: "He entered again into a synagogue; and a man was there whose hand was withered. They were watching Him to see if He would heal him on the Sabbath, so that they might accuse Him" (vv. 1–2).

They're gunning for Him already! Jesus has hardly begun His

ministry, and they are already plotting against Him. The fact that a man afflicted with a withered hand had made his way to Jesus didn't matter to the Pharisees. Neither did his being healed. Their entire focus was on the Sabbath. And there were certain things a good Jew simply did not do on the Sabbath!

I love the way Jesus did what was right, then confronted His critics with a crucial question: "He said to the man with the withered hand, 'Get up and come forward!' And He said to them, 'Is it lawful to do good or to do harm on the Sabbath, to save a life or to kill?' But they kept silent" (vv. 3–4).

Why, of course! Legalists are uneasy when they're exposed. Obviously, they didn't appreciate the question. We need to understand the Pharisees. They're the rule makers—the consummate keepers and enforcers of the Law. They represented first-century legalism in full bloom. They're the guys who hand out photocopies of the church rules to all new members and visitors—and you'd better fulfill them. Those lists of endless regulations became far more important than the Law of Moses! They became masters of the tedious. For example, Moses said, "You shall observe the Sabbath and keep it holy." They added further details . . . stuff like, "And don't even think about walking on the synagogue lawn on the Sabbath, because you'll end up breaking blades of grass, which constitutes work." (Try not to smile as you imagine the absurdity.) No one had the courage to challenge the religious leaders for their blatant abuse of power. No one, that is, until Christ, the Lord of the Sabbath, came along.

Knowing that "the Sabbath was made for man, and not man for the Sabbath" (Mark 2:27), Jesus seized an opportunity to meet a need. Fully aware of His critics' treachery, He asked them if the Sabbath was a day for killing or healing, for doing evil or doing good. Great question, which left them mute.

Filled with righteous indignation against the hypocritical, proud Pharisees and enormous compassion for the crippled man, Jesus did what He had come to do. He restored a wounded sinner. The Pharisees growled in disapproval. In absolute defiance Jesus had broken one of their stupid man-made rules they viewed as more important than ministry. And they hated Him for it. Misunderstanding His actions, they didn't appreciate that Jesus colored outside the lines. They demanded that everybody stay within the rigid requirements of their squint-eyed, legalistic religion. Sadly, we still have a bunch of little Pharisees running around our churches today, who get their underwear in a wad when folks fail to fall in line—their line. People like that *never* understand people of grace.

Misunderstood by His Own People

Read a little further in Mark 3 and you come to another crossroad of misunderstanding. Jesus meets a group of people who had gathered as He entered His hometown. Though there is some debate as to whether this was Nazareth or Capernaum, I believe it was Jesus's adopted home of Capernaum, about thirty miles from Nazareth. The folks here remember Jesus as a youngster, tagging along with His parents. They were curious about His newfound fame and, no doubt, came for a firsthand look. The Scriptures tell the story better than I.

> And He came home, and the crowd gathered again, to such an extent that they could not even eat a meal. When His own people heard of this, they went out to take custody of Him; for they were saying, "He has lost his senses." (vv. 20–21)

I must interrupt long enough to interject a thought. Hometown people never understand how a local boy could gain a big following. Like the country-western song says, they always think of you as still being sixteen. In spite of Jesus's unprecedented popularity, these people just couldn't figure that out. Let's trace the growth of His popularity through the first couple of chapters of Mark's Gospel.

First we read, "Immediately the news about Him spread every-where into all the surrounding district of Galilee." That's Mark 1:28. Only a few verses later Mark adds, "When evening came, after the sun had set, they began bringing to Him all who were ill and those who were demon-possessed. And the whole city had gathered at the door" (vv. 32–33). Later, in chapter 2, Mark describes another remarkable scene complete with a burgeoning crowd: "When He had come back to Capernaum several days afterward, it was heard that He was at home. And many were gathered together, so that there was no longer room, not even near the door; and He was speaking the word to them" (vv. 1–2).

The crowd kept coming, and the numbers increased. By the time Jesus was back in Capernaum and met the man with the withered hand (Mark 3), the whole region had heard of this hometown preacher. And talk about a busy schedule! Mark makes it clear that Jesus's involvement with the needs of people had become so consuming, He couldn't even take time to eat (v. 20).

The people could not understand Jesus's obvious obsession with ministry. They were embarrassed for Him. So they decided to put Him away. Why? Because (are you ready?) they were convinced, "He has lost His senses." The Greek suggests, "He is beside Himself." Put bluntly, they determined Jesus was insane. How's that for misunderstanding? You're serving God with sincerity of heart and with great diligence, and your own people think you're nuts.

They no doubt believed the same about the men Christ chose to lead. Andrew and Peter? Not exactly specimens of genius and distinction! These guys were fishermen turned religious fanatics. They left a profitable business to join this itinerant gospel bandwagon. Neither one of them could have had both oars in the water. And these were the guys Jesus was hanging out with. So the townspeople thought, *Let's just put Him away. He'll come to His senses after some time back home.* They missed the point. They completely misunderstood. To them Christ's passion hung somewhere between fanaticism and insanity.

I'm told that the closer Thomas Edison came to inventing the incandescent light, the less he ate and slept. Meals were left untouched. Lamps in his shop remained lit for days. Yet, after more than seven hundred failed experiments, Edison's dream of an incandescent light became reality. Every time you and I flip a light switch we ought to say, "Thanks, Mr. Edison. You did it. You stayed at it and I'll never be in the dark." But the people in Edison's day? They grew a little concerned about him too. He was viewed as eccentric; some felt he was borderline insane. With greatness comes misunderstanding.

It wouldn't hurt to put yourself in the shoes of someone viewed by others as beside themselves when they're not. Make it personal. Can you imagine the pain of being called insane? Or, to take it a step further, can you imagine the horror of being admitted to a mental hospital when you're healthier than the people around you? Jesus felt all of that. He was completely misunderstood by His own people. But that was not the end. It's one thing to be thought insane. It's even worse to be called demonic.

Misunderstood by the Scribes

Along came the scribes. The first group misunderstood Jesus's actions. The second group misunderstood His passion. Now these people misunderstand His power. A group of scribes from Jerusalem made their way to Capernaum. And as they traveled, Mark tells us, they "were saying, 'He is possessed by Beelzebub,' and 'He casts out the demons by the ruler of the demons'" (Mark 3:22).

Now I've had my share of criticisms and misunderstandings, but I'm grateful I've never been criticized for that one (that I'm aware of!). Think of the sting of being called Satan. Jesus answered the scribes' wild accusations. With powerful logic He systematically disarmed their inaccurate assault. If He were Satan, how could He cast out demons from His own realm? A kingdom divided against itself would be no kingdom at all. Read Mark 3:24–29 for yourself, and you'll see the power in His response. The scribes misunderstood Jesus's power, dismissing Him as demonic.

A brief warning is appropriate here. Harsh words can hit and stick like shrapnel in the mind. Tragically, a victim might spend the better part of a lifetime trying to get the brain to unload it. Whoever thought up the saying, "Sticks and stones may break my bones but words will never hurt me," ought to be drawn and quartered. Nothing could be further from reality. Unfair names and ugly words do harm us, and that harm can be permanent. We need to guard what we say about other people, especially to our children and loved ones.

Though fully God Himself, Jesus was human too. That charge must have stung and cut deep into His human emotions. But that's what happens when misunderstandings occur. In the heat of the moment the assailant goes for your character. And it hurts . . . deeply. Jesus entered Galilee doing remarkable miracles on behalf of the neediest people only to hear His critics call Him evil. We can only imagine how that would feel. You might expect such harsh words from your enemies, but from your *own family*?

Misunderstood by His Family

The worst of the four blows that Jesus endured came from His own blood relatives. How difficult it must have been when He was misunderstood by His immediate family.

> Then His mother and His brothers arrived, and standing outside they sent word to Him and called Him. A crowd was sitting around Him, and they said to Him, "Behold, Your mother and Your brothers are outside looking for You." Answering them, He said, "Who are My mother and My brothers?" Looking about at those who were sitting around Him, He said, "Behold My mother and My brothers! For whoever does the will of God, he is My brother and sister and mother." (Mark 3:31–35)

After careful study I'm convinced that the family members Mark mentions here waited outside and called for Him because they believed Jesus was demented. They wanted to spare Him shame and protect Him from further public ridicule.

A. T. Robertson writes of this being a "pathetic picture of the mother and brothers standing on the outside of the house, thinking that Jesus inside is beside himself and wanting to take Him home."[2]

Have you known the pain of your own family turning on you because they misunderstood you? It's what I would call the heartache of an inside attack. It's terrible. It dislodges your deepest roots and demoralizes you. In some cases you never fully recover. It is, I feel, misunderstanding of the most painful sort.

How utterly wrong Jesus's mother and brothers were. They completely misjudged Him. On top of that, they attempted to mishandle Him. Realizing their failure to understand, Jesus refused to go out to them. His higher priority was with those who had gathered around Him to hear what He had to say, to receive what He came to bring.

For you who have experienced a painful family misunderstanding, be very gentle in how you speak to your offenders, especially if they're your parents or parents-in-law. A strange theory emerged many years ago that repudiated the value of respecting parents, especially when they're in the wrong. Until you've been a parent for a number of years, you'll not realize the difficulty and pain you caused when you blew it with your kids. My advice is simple: tread lightly. Consider much of that relationship as sacred ground, even if you're right.

Jesus resisted going out and rebuking His mother and other family members in public. He kept right on doing what He was doing, leaving them to figure things out for themselves.

That must have been one of the most painful experiences during Jesus's early ministry—to have His own family publicly turn on Him. Yet, in spite of being misunderstood, He endured. You can too.

HELP TO GET YOU THROUGH

Let me give you a little help on getting through the tough stuff of personal misunderstanding. Three simple thoughts come to mind. Because they have worked for me, I offer them to you.

When misunderstood, ask, "who?" This is the age-old advice of considering the source. Jesus, in these various circumstances, saw Himself through other people's eyes. Each time that helped Him grasp why they saw Him as they did and how He should respond. Asking, "who?" is a good place to start.

If misunderstanding continues, ask, "why?" You may be misunderstood because of something you're doing inadvertently. We all have blind spots that keep us from seeing the whole picture . . . the way others see us. If you are often misunderstood on the same point, you'd be wise to examine *why*. We all need to examine ourselves from time to time. Asking why is healthy.

When misunderstanding is resolved, ask, "what?" What can you learn from the experience? Could you have responded to the situation in a more mature manner? Have you owned your mistakes? Are you sure there are no other bases to cover? Learning from misunderstanding can help prevent future pain and anguish.

I will close this chapter with two important words: *forgiveness* and *bitterness*. Without the first you'll limp through life with the second. Misunderstanding can breed deep-seated bitterness, which doesn't easily go away. Forgiveness must occur if you ever hope to be free of your painful past. It does not mean you agree. It doesn't necessarily mean you now have a close relationship with your offender. But it does mean you let it go . . . forever. And yes, to forgive *does* mean to forget. Bitterness deposits dangerous germs in our memory banks. It can cause disease that lingers and robs us of joy and peace as the years stack up. So you must forgive and forget. Bitterness replaces forgiveness, or forgiveness erases bitterness. They cannot coexist.

If you're reading these words and realize you're consumed with bitterness, I urge you to come to terms with it and let it go. You cannot change the past, but your bitterness can change you. You must deliberately pursue forgiveness. There will be other collision courses with misunderstanding, just like the hockey game I mentioned earlier. They will burst upon you again and again, and your bitterness will only intensify, until you come to the place of full forgiveness. And you will find, when you collide again with a misunderstanding person, you can handle it—you can let it go.

Remember Emerson's words? "To be great is to be misunderstood." Here's a better statement: "To be greater is to forgive the one who misunderstood."

✧

Our Father, we realize that it is impossible to get through the tough stuff of misunderstanding on our own. Only You can make it happen . . . And how great it is when that happens! We realize that this kind of greatness begins and ends with You. Bring us to the place where we can live as Your Son lived, facing head-on those who misunderstand us, hearing their words and feeling the sting of their accusations and even insults, but learning how to live above them. Take these few words from this chapter and etch them into our hearts, bringing new hope and needed refreshment. Help us to fully forgive. I ask this especially for the one whose life is being consumed by the acid of resentment and crippled by the misery of bitterness. Bring us full circle, Father, to a place of complete relief, where no matter who may have misunderstood us, we are able to go on, like Your Son went on . . . all the way to the cross.

In His triumphant name, I pray. Amen.

Three

Getting Through the Tough Stuff of Anxiety

WHAT'S MAKING YOU BITE YOUR NAILS THESE DAYS? I don't mean the little foxes that nibble away at your mind. I'm not referring to those unimportant intruders that interrupt your day like a dripping faucet, a misplaced set of keys, or a flat tire in the morning. I'm referring to the ulcer-causing, big-time, mental monsters that crawl into your head, then go with you to bed and steal your sleep. Also there are the relentless worries that take away the delight of a much-needed weekend holiday. I have in mind those dread concerns you can't shake off. Does anything make you anxious like that?

Several years ago the National Anxiety Center in Maplewood, New Jersey, released the "Top Ten Anxieties for the 1990s." They were (1) AIDS, (2) drug abuse, (3) nuclear waste, (4) the ozone layer,

(5) famine, (6) the homeless, (7) the federal deficit, (8) air pollution, (9) water pollution, and (10) garbage. Since then, in the light of September 11, 2001, the Center has revised its list to put "global terrorism" as the leading source of anxiety. Moreover, the Center's founder, Alan Caruba, notes that "the 1990s list primarily was intended to reflect the environmental and social issues of that decade."[1] Today, obviously, we would add the fear of a terrorist attack, the worries of a full-scale war, the threat of nuclear attack from North Korea or China, the risk of losing a good job, and maybe the disquieting thoughts of growing old alone and unwanted.

Interestingly, while we all have different lists, our deep, relentless worries carry a similar effect. They make us uneasy. They steal smiles from our faces. They cast dark shadows on our futures by spotlighting our shameful pasts. Stubborn anxieties work like petty thieves in the dark corners of our thoughts as they pickpocket our peace and kidnap our joy.

Left to do its insidious work, anxiety will eventually drain us of all resources and leave us emotionally bankrupt and spiritually immobilized, which is why the tough stuff of anxiety must be confronted head-on. The first step in that process is to analyze and understand its power.

AN OVERVIEW OF ANXIETY

Throughout my more than forty years of pastoral ministry, whenever I've taught or spoken on the topic of anxiety, I've always highlighted the relevant counsel of the apostle Paul in his letter to the Philippians. Type in the words *worry* or *anxiety* into the search engine of my heart, and Philippians 4 quickly flashes on my mind.

What Anxiety Is

For some critical clues to the nature of anxiety, let's look closely at that first-century shepherd's calming words, which he addresses to a group of anxious sheep.

> Rejoice in the Lord always; again I will say, rejoice! Let your gentle spirit be known to all men. The Lord is near. Be anxious for nothing, but in everything by prayer and supplication with thanksgiving let your requests be made known to God. And the peace of God, which surpasses all comprehension, will guard your hearts and minds in Christ Jesus. (Philippians 4:4–7)

Immediately we discover a four-word command that could be rendered, literally, "Stop worrying about anything!" The word translated "anxious" comes from the Greek verb *merimnaō*, meaning "to be divided or distracted." In Latin the same word is translated *anxius*, which carries the added nuance of choking or strangling. The word also appears in German as *wurgen*, from which we derive our English word *worry*. The tough stuff of anxiety threatens to strangle the life out of us, leaving us asphyxiated by fear and gasping for hope.

Jesus used similar terms when He referred to worry in His parable of the sower in Mark 4. The Master Illustrator painted a picture in the minds of His listeners of a farmer sowing seed in four types of soil. In that parable He mentions a seed being sown among thorns. While doing so He underscores both the real nature and the destructive power of anxiety. Jesus said, "Other seed fell among the thorns, and the thorns came up and *choked it,* and it yielded no crop" (v. 7; emphasis added). Later, when the disciples asked Jesus about the meaning of the parable, He interpreted His own words. Regarding the seed sown among thorns, He explained, "And others are the ones on whom seed was sown among the thorns; these are the ones who have heard the word, but the *worries* of the world, and the deceitfulness of riches, and desires for other things enter in and *choke* the word, and it becomes unfruitful" (vv. 18–19; emphasis added).

The One planting the seed sowed the Word. Clearly the Sower would be Jesus and His teaching, but the reference would also include anyone sowing truth through teaching or preaching. The soil would be the hearts and minds of all who hear the truth as it is being sown. Anxiety sprouts like weeds and thorns, grows up around the truth of God's Word, choking away the life and peace it can bring. In a graphic lesson concerning seeds and soil Jesus makes a direct connection between the devastating effects of anxiety and those of strangulation. It chokes us!

What Anxiety Does

I have my own definition for anxiety. *Anxiety is the painful uneasiness of the mind that feeds on impending fears.* In its mildest form we simply churn. In its most severe form we panic. This is a good place to pause and dig deeper. Why is anxiety so wrong and spiritually debilitating? I want to offer three statements that help answer that question. Hopefully they will serve as a springboard for an illustration from biblical days.

Anxiety highlights the human viewpoint and strangles the divine, so we become fearful. When we worry, we have such a high level of awareness of the human events surrounding us that God's perspective gets choked out. Worry strangles the divine perspective from our daily living, which puts us on edge.

Anxiety chokes our ability to distinguish the incidental from the essen-

tial, so we get distracted. In the midst of the worrisome details, we add endless fears, doubts, tasks, expectations, and pressures. Eventually we lose focus on what matters. We become distracted by incidentals and, at the same time, neglect the essentials. Fruitful people are usually relaxed people. Unproductive people, on the other hand, are tied up in knots, having allowed incidental worries to entangle their minds like a thorny vine which leads to distraction.

Anxiety siphons our joy and makes us judgmental rather than accepting of others, so we become negative. We become negative when worry wins the battle. Inevitably we take our anxiety out on others. Worry works like bad cholesterol, hardening the arteries of our spiritual hearts and clogging the flow of love and grace toward people. Eventually, as the thorns and thistles intensify, we grow to become negative, bitter, and narrow and basically of little good to anyone.

In those tough times, when anxiety creeps in filling our minds with fear, distraction, and bitterness, we must turn to the One who offers an unexplainable peace. Thankfully we're not alone in this struggle. And neither were those closest to Jesus while He was on earth. There is one biblical scene where Jesus appears as a gentle and compassionate Teacher offering perspective and correction to a fretting friend.

A FIRST-CENTURY PORTRAIT OF ANXIETY

The scene I have in mind is recorded in Luke 10. It is one of the most intimate vignettes from the life of Jesus. The setting is the home of three of our Lord's closest friends—Martha, Mary, and Lazarus—who lived in the village of Bethany just outside Jerusalem.

For various undisclosed reasons Jesus chose their home as a place of refuge, an ideal retreat away from the strain and press of public ministry. It was here He found safe harbor among people who didn't ask leading questions, who accepted Him as He was, who were not overtly critical, and who didn't have hidden agendas. When I read this story, I wonder to myself if Jesus lived on earth today, would He choose *my* home? While I'm at it, would *your* home be one of those places where He'd find relaxation and relief?

Let's again allow the Scriptures to recast the poignant scene. Observe closely as these three unsuspecting individuals react to a visit from their famous friend and some of His weary and hungry disciples.

> Now as they were traveling along, He entered a village; and a woman named Martha welcomed Him into her home. She had a sister called Mary, who was seated at the Lord's feet, listening to His word. But Martha was distracted with all her preparations; and she came up to Him and said, "Lord, do You not care that my sister has left me to do all the serving alone? Then tell her to help me." But the Lord answered and said to her, "Martha, Martha, you are worried and bothered about so many things; but only one thing is necessary, for Mary has chosen the good part, which shall not be taken away from her." (Luke 10:38–42)

Before I proceed, perhaps a disclaimer or two is in order.

I need to make clear that Martha's name has no general significance. Neither does her gender. The person who gives in to such anxiety-producing distractions could have any name . . . and could be a man or a woman. Young or old. Rich or bankrupt.

I must also point out that Martha is not our only concern. We want to look closely at the entire story and all the characters involved. God has designed His creation with a mysterious and wonderful variety of temperaments and personalities. Some folks are dreamy and artsy, while others enjoy poring over procedures and flow charts. Some folks live for details; others insist on the bigger picture. You get the idea.

John Trent and Gary Smalley use four animals to describe four different temperaments people possess.[2]

1. *Otters* are the fun-loving, easygoing folks among us. They always enjoy themselves and exude a carefree attitude toward just about every situation. My wife, Cynthia, reminds me I'm an otter. She has said that this personality has its benefits, but if I were in charge of the picnic there would be only balloons! Otters hang loose.

2. *Lions*, in contrast, take charge. At the party they make certain everyone gets a party hat, a piece of cake, *and* a name tag.

3. *Golden retrievers* are those relational, pleasant folks whom you'd want with you in a pinch. Loyalty and compassion are high on the list of priorities with golden retriever-types.

4. Then there are the *beavers*, scampering around, working hard, sticking their noses into everything and making sure all the details are covered. They're borderline obsessive about minutia. They're those detail-minded people who point out misspellings in church bulletins and correct the preacher's grammar.

This might be a stretch, but I think Martha was a mixture—part lion and part beaver. She was delighted to see Jesus, to be sure, but when she did, she immediately realized she had a huge job on her hands. There was a meal to cook, a table to set, and guests to make comfortable. That required serious planning and efficient execution. No one can fault Martha for diligence.

Mary, however, fell somewhere between a retriever and an otter. Understanding the rarity of the moment of just being in His presence, Mary sat like a loyal lapdog basking in her Master's shadow.

She didn't view the day as a project to tackle but as an intimate moment to enjoy. Nothing's right or wrong about either temperament, unless they're taken to the extreme. And that's what Jesus confronted in Martha.

Luke's story offers an eloquent study in contrast. After Martha met Jesus at the door (Luke 10:38), she must have gone straight to work preparing the meal. We know that because Luke moves quickly to describe what Mary did. He writes, "She had a sister called Mary, who was seated at the Lord's feet, listening to His word" (v. 39).

When Jesus showed up unexpectedly, Mary chose to seize the moment, stop everything, and listen to His teaching. But Martha "was distracted with all her preparations" (v. 40). In other words, Mary seized the opportunity, but Martha, anxious and distracted, missed it. Perhaps she couldn't help herself. After all, she was likely the oldest. (I've said for years that parents owe their oldest child one thing: *an apology!* All their lives we've put them into the mold of having to step up and take charge.) Not surprisingly, Martha is acting responsibly. Unfortunately she is so responsible that she gets everything else out of focus.

Martha reached her boiling point and in a moment of exasperation blurted, "Lord, do You not care that my sister has left me to do all the serving alone? Then tell her to help me" (v. 40).

I have a feeling she spoke those words to Jesus while frowning and glaring at her younger sister, Mary. Hands on hips, brow beaded with sweat, Martha likely stomped her foot in protest. Lions do a lot of foot stomping.

That scene reminds me of words my friend Jeanne Hendricks wrote in her book *A Woman for All Seasons.* In a chapter she calls "The Tale of Two Sisters," Jeanne describes a similar experience from her own kitchen several years ago.

Frustration is a very real problem. Some years ago I was hosting a Thanksgiving dinner in our little home, which happened to be short on kitchen counter space. The Lord and I had many conversations about the fact that the house was too small, but He kept saying, "Wait," and I was doing the best I could—I thought.

Shortly before it was time to serve the meal, I slipped into the hot kitchen to check on my roasting turkey. As I was lifting it from one place to another in a space too tight for efficient operation, it slipped and fell right down on the floor! Two thoughts flashed: (1) the floor's clean, and (2) nobody's here. I grabbed it and lifted it to the platter, grateful that no one had witnessed my clumsiness. Suddenly I felt a surge of self-pity. I leaned up against the wall and tears of frustration came to my eyes. In my heart I said, "Lord, I told You so! Now look what's happened! It's all Your fault!"

Then I heard laughter and talking from the other room and I suddenly felt ashamed. What if somebody should come and see me crumpled in such dejection? I grabbed newspaper to put over the mess on the floor and decided I would have it out with the Lord later. I think I know a little of how Martha felt. [3]

Martha's out-of-balance concerns over the meal preparations prevented her from focusing on Jesus. Because her anxiety had gotten the best of her, she missed a potentially life-altering encounter with the Savior. The stress she brought onto herself strangled her ability to relish Christ's words and experience the quiet benefit of His presence.

I love how our Lord responds. He gently addressed her, "Martha, Martha." Gentle Jesus, gracious and calm. He didn't deliver a thundering lecture, wagging His finger in Martha's face. He didn't throw open the family Bible and shame her into reading ten verses aloud. None of that. I'm convinced He felt compassion for Martha. He could have even wrapped His strong arms around her and whispered, "You are worried and bothered about so many things; but only one thing is necessary, for Mary has chosen the good part, which shall not be taken away from her" (vv. 41–42).

Jesus pinpointed Martha's trouble. She had allowed the anxiety of the moment to cloud her attitude and steal her joy. Often that twisted mindset shows up plain as day on our grimacing faces. I wonder if Martha's body language betrayed her internal stress.

Mary had chosen a better way—the way of life and peace found at the feet of Jesus. For the rest of her life she would be able to remember those precious hours with her beloved Savior. Martha may have known only frustration and regret had not Jesus lovingly rebuked her.

ANXIETY . . . UP CLOSE AND PERSONAL

After years of studying the tough stuff of anxiety (and yielding to it more times than I want to remember), I've distilled what I've learned about its destructive power into four practical principles. They may seem negative at first glance, but when embraced and acted on, they can become powerful antidotes against the sting of anxiety. I'll make them easy to remember by giving them to you in simple math— addition, subtraction, multiplication, and division.

We worry when we add *unnecessary pressure to an already full plate.* This is the most common error busy people make. It's the addition that defeats us! We worry when we add the pressure of exterior image, when we increase the pace to keep up with the Joneses, when we intensify our emotional responsibility in response to someone else's struggle. We worry when we add unreasonable expectations of others. I've personally struggled with that one over the years. As a pastor I used to worry about living up to the expectations of so many people. What a terrible way to live or to minister!

Anxiety lurks in those trumped-up expectations so common in local church ministry. There's enough otter in me to want to please everyone and enough retriever in me to worry when I don't. I don't enjoy criticism, but I receive it. Trying to meet everyone's expectations adds unnecessary pressure. Thankfully during the past ten years or so the Lord has helped me to put that to rest. Worrying about such things made me angry at myself. Angry at God's people. Angry at ministry. Through the power of His Word and the gracious assistance of His Spirit, God helped release me from the jagged jaws of worrying about pleasing people. You and I worry when we add things to a plate of cares already full. Adding makes us angry.

We worry when we subtract *God's presence from our crises.* We worry when we forget God's presence and God's sovereignty. We worry when we subtract His timing from our plans. When we eliminate prayer from our daily routines. When we subtract divine perspective from tough times. Anxiety overcomes us when we subtract God's infinite power from our own feeble initiatives.

The late Peter Marshall, renowned chaplain of the United States Senate, prayed, "Father . . . check our impulse to spread ourselves so thin that we are exposed to fear and doubt, to the weariness and impatience that makes our tempers wear thin, that robs us of peace of mind, that makes skies gray when they should be blue, that stifles a song along the corridor of our hearts."[4]

The seasoned pastor understood the peril of leaving God out of life's more difficult equations. Adversity minus God's presence equals doubt and fear. Every time. Our songs are stifled from the corridors of our hearts. Subtracting makes us doubtful.

We worry when we multiply *our problems by inserting our solutions prematurely.* When we insert our solutions too rapidly, complications set in. And then we worry when our so-called solutions fail. Anxiety grips us when we insist on finding a way out of the tough stretches in life instead of taking God's path through them. We also give in to anxiety when we multiply our fears with wild imaginations. Always thinking the worst makes us irrational and afraid, like a child hearing noises in his closet or monsters under his bed. Our imaginations often run wild in the midst of tough times, and the resulting fear can be paralyzing. Multiplying makes us fearful.

We worry when we divide *life into the secular and the sacred.* God doesn't want to compartmentalize our lives. He wants every aspect to be under His control. Selective trust makes us forget His everyday provisions. The less we allow Him to be part of our every day, the more anxious we become. How easy it is to tell ourselves that *this* part is in the realm of God's concern, but not *that*. Wrong! Dividing life into sacred and secular categories makes us forget His goodness. Dividing makes us forgetful.

Before you move on to the next chapter, it wouldn't hurt you to pause right now and reflect on your list of worries. Take a good look through the current events of your life. What is it that has you anxious? Overcoming those anxious fears won't be as easy as simply sitting in a church service or finding some magical Bible verse. You probably know that. The truth is, no matter what you are facing, worrying will do you more harm than good.

Eugene Peterson has captured Jesus's words in today's terms. Please read the following slowly and aloud. Let them sink in softly and thoughtfully.

If you decide for God, living a life of God-worship, it follows that you don't fuss about what's on the table at mealtimes or whether the clothes in your closet are in fashion. There is far more to your life than the food you put in your stomach, more to your outer appearance than the clothes you hang on your body. Look at the birds, free and unfettered, not tied down to a job description, careless in the care of God. And you count far more to him than birds.

Has anyone, by fussing in front of the mirror ever gotten taller by so much as an inch? All this time and money wasted on fashion—do you think it makes that much difference? Instead of looking at the fashions, walk out into the fields and look at the wildflowers. They never primp or shop, but have you ever seen color and design quite like it? The ten best-dressed men and women in the country look shabby alongside them.

If God gives such attention to the appearance of wild-flowers—most of which are never even seen—don't you think he'll attend to you, take pride in you, do his best for you? What I'm trying to do here is to get you to relax, to not be so pre-occupied with *getting*, so you can respond to God's *giving*. People who don't know God and the way he works fuss over these things, but you know both God and how he works. Steep your life in God-reality, God-initiative, God-provisions. Don't worry about missing out. You'll find all your everyday human concerns will be met.

Give your entire attention to what God is doing right now, and don't get worked up about what may or may not happen tomorrow. God will help you deal with whatever hard things come up when the time comes. (Matthew 6:26–34 MSG)

Worried about tomorrow? Getting strangled on anxieties that you can't seem to dislodge? Feeling a lot like Martha? Jesus invites you to "look at the birds, free and unfettered," and notice that they are "careless in the care of God." Be honest, now don't you think God cares more about you than tiny wrens or sparrows or crows? Absolutely.

So relax. Stop all that worrying about tomorrow . . . or next week . . . or next month. God specializes in getting you through the tough stuff, no matter when it happens.

Four

Getting Through the Tough Stuff of Shame

WHEN IT COMES TO PUBLIC SHAME, few people think of Jesus. If I were to ask you to list the names of twenty people you feel are deserving of shame, you'd probably not include the name Jesus Christ. I'm certainly not suggesting that He is deserving of shame, but we easily forget He experienced it.

The sinless Son of God took all our sins on Himself when He died on the cross. It was there He endured the shame of the world. Every wicked deed done by humanity, He took on Himself when He suffered and died in our place. The horror of Auschwitz, the evils of Stalin and Pol Pot and Saddam Hussein, the atrocities of Rwanda, the silent slaughter of tens of millions of aborted children, the maximum depth of each of our sinful thoughts, and the full extent of our reckless actions—all were piled on Christ at the cross. His death personified shame.

Many who have now seen and felt the power of Mel Gibson's *The*

Passion of the Christ have a renewed appreciation for the depth of shame Christ endured on our behalf during His final, agonizing hours on earth. As all of that came clear to me while watching the film, I found myself sobbing with my head in my hands.

In his volume, *The Execution of Jesus,* William Riley Wilson writes, "Not only was the cross the most painful of deaths, it was also considered the most debasing. The condemned man was stripped naked and left exposed in his agony, and often the Romans even denied burial to the victim, allowing his body to hang on the cross until it disintegrated. It is understandable that, according to Jewish law, anyone who was crucified was considered cursed."[1]

To be cursed is to suffer shame. Twelfth-century monk Bernard of Clairvaux described it this way:

> O sacred Head, now wounded,
> With grief and shame weighed down,
> Now scornfully surrounded
> With thorns thine only crown;
> How pale art Thou with anguish,
> With sore abuse and scorn,
> How does that visage languish,
> Which once was bright as morn! [2]

PUBLIC SHAME EXPLORED AND EXAMINED

The old monk understood that there is often agony and cruelty connected with shame. Shame runs deeper than guilt. Guilt typically remains a private affair. We learn to keep those inner indictments to ourselves, safely out of public view. But the tough stuff of shame follows you wherever you go like a bad rap sheet. Shame straps you to your torturous past, putting everything on display. Private shame—

the shame that comes from years of physical or sexual abuse, or the lonely suffering that emerges from disabilities such as speech impediments, anxiety or eating disorders, a prison sentence or time spent in a mental institution or a rehab clinic—pushes victims to the corners of the room, into the shadows of society. Shame becomes a relentless, accusing voice that whispers, "You are worthless! You don't mean anything to anyone! You're totally unworthy! You will never amount to anything! You blew it! You're finished!"

Shame penetrates deeper than embarrassment; it cuts wider than disappointment. Its scars are ugly and often permanent. Being the lowest form of self-hatred, shame has driven many people slumping under its burden to retreat into a sort of living death, which ultimately ends in suicide.

Shame keeps a young mother chained to her emotionally traumatic past, bruised and battered sexually by her drunken father.

Shame haunts a middle-aged woman expected by others to "move on" in her life following her husband's reckless affair and their subsequent bitter divorce.

Shame assails a teenager lost in a world of confusion and seclusion brought about by his or her inability to learn as quickly as others and compete with peers.

Shame holds back a child born with a deformity or disability from experiencing the carefree joys of recess and field trips.

Shame assaults the church leader caught in an illicit relationship with one of his parishioners and forced to confess his sin publicly.

A man I now respect and consider a friend experienced the depth of that intense shame. He was once an honored pastor with a good marriage and a fine family. But there existed a shadowy twist to his story. Eventually it came to light that he was involved sexually with one of his church members. Found out, he stood before the church and confessed his sin and felt the depth of public shame.

Years later, in a conversation he and I had about that awful period of his life, he said, "I don't know that I have words to describe the shame my family and I experienced. I found that I could negotiate my way around guilt, but I could not rationalize shame. My wife and I still look back on that dark day, calling it 'Black Sunday.'" Along with his wife and children, he felt what few people ever do—the painful alienation of public shame. To this day, tears are near the surface when that dark day is mentioned.

The tough stuff of shame can't simply be sloughed off. There remains a lingering disgrace that holds us tightly in its grip.

But that bottomless despair does not have to be our lot indefinitely. The scars need not be permanent. Christ desires to meet us in those dark corners and lift us to safety by redeeming our dignity and worth. His grace is greater than our shame. Where sin abounds, grace superabounds! He becomes for us our personal shame-bearer who walks with us through those harsh, agonizing days when we feel most alone and afraid. How can He do that? Remember, He's been there. He has felt the aches of indignity and humiliation. In fact, there's no limit to the depth of shame He can see us through, because there's no limit to the grace He can supply.

Travel back with me to a first-century scene. Jesus confronts a broken and humiliated woman ensnared in the most shameful of circumstances. We are allowed to watch as He rescues her from the jagged edge of shame's powerful jaws.

An Adulteress and Her Accusers

A nameless woman takes center stage in one of the most poignant scenes in all the New Testament. There, in the midst of her sin, she encountered Jesus, the Savior of the world. She assumed that her deeds done in the dark would never be known in the light. Hers was a shameful, secret sin. Then one day she came face to face with Jesus, the spotless Lamb of God, whose penetrating gaze looked squarely on her disgrace.

We are indebted to one of Jesus's original disciples, John, for including this narrative as part of his record of Christ's ministry to the broken people of Judah. Read carefully as he describes this unusually delicate scene.

> Early in the morning He came again into the temple, and all the people were coming to Him; and He sat down and began to teach them. The scribes and the Pharisees brought a woman caught in adultery, and having set her in the center of the court, they said to Him, "Teacher, this woman has been caught in adultery, in the very act. Now in the Law Moses commanded us to stone such women; what then do you say?" They were saying this, testing Him, so that they might have grounds for accusing Him. But Jesus stooped down, and with His finger wrote on the ground. But when they persisted in asking Him, He straightened up, and said to them, "He who is without sin among you, let him be the first to throw a stone at her." Again He stooped down and wrote on the ground. And when they heard it, they began to go out one by one, beginning with the older ones, and He was left alone, and the woman, where she was, in the center of the court. Straightening up, Jesus said to her, "Woman, where are they? Did no one condemn you?" And she said, "No one, Lord." And Jesus said, "I do not condemn you either. Go. From now on sin no more." (John 8:1–11)

You have just read one of the most remarkable dramas in the entire Bible. We can only imagine what it would have been like to have been a bug on the wall of that temple, watching it unfold.

It all began early in the morning when Jerusalem lay damp with dew. Long purple shadows fell among the temple columns. Songbirds chirped in the low-hanging trees. Several people joined in what we would call today a small-group Bible study, to be taught by the One who taught as no other. They had come to hear the words of the thirty-something teacher from Nazareth. He was young, but He had wisdom beyond His years. They had no idea what they would hear from Him that morning. A crowd had gathered in the temple court to hear Jesus; no doubt many spent the night on the cool ground to make certain they could sit up close. In rabbinical fashion Jesus sat down with them as He began to teach.

Suddenly a regimen of stern-faced scribes and Pharisees interrupted Jesus, dragging a disheveled woman across the pavement and into the great hall. The people must have gasped in disbelief at the spectacle. Jesus rose to His feet and faced the self-righteous brigade of clerics and their humiliated prisoner in tow. They were the grace-killing legalists of Israel, all spit-shined and polished for another day's work of judging and criticizing others. They had come to make a public example of someone who didn't belong in their midst. Not a man, but a woman. But not just any woman . . . a lady of the night who had just been in bed with a man who wasn't her husband. They had actually caught her in the act.

The woman—never named by John or anyone else in the story—must have stood trembling like an abused dog, muzzled by fear. Her head was bowed, her hair disheveled, her clothing torn. Shame was written across her face. Her accusers planned to use her to trap Jesus. They loathed Him and His teaching and especially His growing popularity. They hated His grace most of all. Their goal was to get Him killed, whatever it took. What they were doing on this morning was all part of a diabolical plan to rid themselves and the land of the menacing prophet from Nazareth.

The religious leaders abruptly addressed Jesus. "Teacher, this woman has been caught in adultery, in the very act. Now, in the Law Moses commanded us to stone such women; what then do You say?" Interestingly they invoked the name of Moses before they leveled the charge.

That was part of the trap. They'd haul this pitiful woman in front of Jesus and a crowd of wide-eyed people, claim the authority of Moses, and then ask sneering, "What then do You say?" British author William Barclay writes:

> The Scribes and Pharisees were out to get some charge on which they could discredit Jesus; and here they thought they had impaled Him inescapably on the horns of a dilemma. When a difficult legal question arose, the natural and routine thing was to take it to a rabbi for a decision. So the Scribes and Pharisees approached Jesus as a rabbi.[3]

The Mishnah, Judaism's handbook of religious tradition, minced no words. It mandated that a man caught in adultery was to be strangled and placed knee-deep in dung, with a towel wrapped around his neck so the rope wouldn't break his skin. A woman caught in the act of adultery faced public stoning. Moses had written in the Law that if the act occurred in a city, both the man and woman were to be stoned. Was this particular woman guilty? Absolutely. They apparently caught her in the very act of sexual intercourse. The Greek word translated "caught" literally means "to seize" or "to overcome," suggesting that her accusers themselves found her in the very act of adultery and apprehended her while still in bed with her partner. But what about the man? Had he escaped? Likely not, since the religious leaders would have easily outnumbered him. My suspicions prompt me to suggest that he was a coconspirator (maybe one of them!), who had been put up to the lurid tryst beforehand. A conspiracy is not out of the question, knowing the wickedness of the accusers' hearts. The trembling woman in disarray, humiliated in front of the morning Bible study group, was nothing more than half a small piece of bait used to capture bigger game. They had Jesus in their sights. They cared nothing about the woman or her future. At that moment she meant nothing to them or to anyone else for that matter—no one except Jesus.

The unflappable young Teacher stood silently and stared, studying the entire scene. I find it remarkable that Jesus often said more in His silence than with His words. There's wisdom in remaining quiet at such crucial moments when charges are flying and tempers are flaring. But Jesus knew the hearts of these men. He read their motive like an open book. He sensed their deliberate attempt to catch Him unprepared and snare Him with His own words.

Consider quickly the options. Had Jesus immediately agreed to the stoning, they could have accused Him of hypocrisy. A man who had been teaching the importance of compassion and forgiveness would not allow such a harsh penalty. In addition, had Jesus made that call, He could have been charged with treason. Only a Roman official could determine the verdict of death on an individual. Jesus would have had no legal authority to have her stoned to death.

On the other hand, had He simply demanded she be forgiven and set free, they would have pounced on Him for condoning sin and ignoring the Law of Moses.

Choosing neither option, according to John's narrative, "Jesus stooped down and with His finger wrote on the ground." The only time in all Scripture where we're told Jesus wrote anything is here in this scene. But what did He write? There are some who believe Jesus simply scribbled in the dust as He was collecting His thoughts. Yet the Greek word translated "wrote" suggests something more.

I believe John was an eyewitness. Writing now toward the end of the first century, he recorded that Jesus *wrote* in the sand. The Greek term John uses, which the English renders as "wrote," is *katagraphō*. The last half of that word, *graphō*, is the verb "to write." The Greek prefix *kata* can mean "against." In other words, I'm suggesting that John intended to show that Jesus wrote something in the sand that would have been incriminating to the religious leaders. Perhaps He actually did write something "against" them. Could it be that Jesus stooped and began to write out the sins of the woman's accusers in letters large enough for them and others to read? Pause and picture the scene as each accuser reads his own sins written in the sand. We cannot say for sure that this is what occurred, but if it did, can you imagine their surprise?

WHO OR WHAT CONDEMNS YOU?

The silence was broken by the words Jesus spoke. Where there remains some ambiguity as to exactly what He wrote in the sand, there's no doubt about the meaning of what He said. As the scribes and Pharisees frowned and stared, John tells us Jesus rose to His feet and said to them, "He who is without sin among you, let him be the first to throw a stone at her" (v. 7). Talk about shock! Such an incisive answer hit them like a fist in the face.

In fact, the text literally reads, "The sinless one of you, first, on her, let him cast a stone." That's awkward in English, but emphatic in Greek. In so many words, Jesus said, "The first one whom I invite to throw a stone is the sinless one! Be sure you have no sins against you. And then you're qualified to bring shame, accusation, and even death on this woman. Only make sure your hearts are pure and sinless."

An aching, awkward silence followed Christ's stinging reply. A mute void swept across the once snarling pack of junkyard dogs. What a moment!

Peter Marshall captures the scene in a vivid manner:

> Looking into their faces, Christ sees into the yesterdays that lie deep in the pools of memory and conscience. He sees into their very hearts, and that moving finger writes on . . .
> Idolater . . .
>   Liar . . .
>   Drunkard . . .
>   Murderer . . .
>   Adulterer . . .
> There is the thud of stone after stone falling on the pavement. Not many of the Pharisees are left. One by one, they creep away—like animals—slinking into the shadows . . . shuffling off into the crowded streets to lose themselves in the multitudes.[4]

Can you picture it? Can you hear the dull sound of stones hitting hard pavement? Can you feel the humiliation of those who walked away? The apostle John writes, "When they heard it, they began to go out one by one, beginning with the older ones, and He was left alone, and the woman, where she was, in the center of the court" (v. 9).

Wouldn't you love to have been a part of the class that morning?

Jesus, after dismissing the accusers, looked directly into the eyes of a woman full of shame, openly exposed and condemned by her accusers. And if that were not enough, there she stood before the righteous Judge of the universe, guilty of adultery, having broken God's holy law. As she met the gaze of the spotless Savior, we need to realize there has not been in the history of time a more remarkable and striking contrast of character: a woman . . . a man; a sinner . . . the sinless Son of God; the shameful adulteress . . . the Holy One of heaven. Imagine it! Two more different people never stood so close.

It is that which makes the final exchange between them so profound. It is here that grace eclipses shame.

"Straightening up, Jesus said to her, 'Woman, where are they? Did no one condemn you?' She said, 'No one, Lord.' And Jesus said, 'I do not condemn you, either. Go. From now on sin no more'" (vv. 10–11).

The only person on earth qualified to condemn the woman refuses to do so. Instead, He freed her. Could it be that for the first time in her life she stopped condemning herself too? That's what Jesus does for us in the humiliating blast of shame—He delivers us from self-condemnation as He sets us free. Free at last!

To All Weighed Down by Shame

There are times I wish I could wave a magic wand over those weighed down by shame and say, "Shame, be gone!" But it doesn't work like that. However, what Jesus did for this broken woman that morning so many centuries ago, He wants to do for you as well. It won't happen instantly, but given the opportunity to step in and bring relief (as He did with the woman that morning), Jesus can make a profound difference!

Two thoughts linger as we close this chapter on getting through the tough stuff of shame. Here are two simple statements that I'm hoping will help you in your struggle to put your painful memories and shameful thoughts behind you.

First, those most unqualified to condemn you, will. Count on it. Those with hearts heavier than the stones in their hands will be the first to throw them. Stay away from modern-day Pharisees, who love few things more than exposing your sin and rubbing your nose in shame. Make certain you keep plenty of distance between you and those who would throw self-righteous stones at you.

Second, the One most qualified to condemn you, won't. You can count on this as well. Stay close to Him. Because by staying close to Him you will discover that you can recover quicker. Draw near and confess your sin to the One who is qualified to condemn but doesn't. And like the woman, you'll be able to go on with your life enjoying a new freedom and purpose for living.

In John Bunyan's *The Pilgrim's Progress* young Christian walks his journey carrying a heavy burden on his back. The burden is sin—all his shameful past. The weight is bound to him with strings tight and strong. He can find no relief. Shame and disgrace along with self-condemnation weigh down on his frame. Finally, at long last he comes to the Wicket Gate. He opens the gate and follows a narrow path which leads to the precipice. There he encounters Jesus Christ, the only One qualified to condemn him, yet He doesn't. Christian gazes across a vast chasm and sees in the distance a barren cross and nearby, an empty tomb. While watching and meditating on the cross and the tomb, the burden that has been bound tightly to him begins to loosen. A song of freedom fills his grateful heart:

> Thus far I did come laden with my sin;
> Nor could ought ease the grief that I was in,
> Till I came hither: What a place is this!

Must here be the beginning of my bliss?
Must here the Burden fall from off my back?
Must here the strings that bound it to me crack?
Blest Cross! Blest sepulcher! Blest rather be
The Man that there was put to Shame for me![5]

What will it take to bring you to such a defining moment? Do I make light of your sin? Not for a moment. Your sin and mine nailed Jesus to that cross. Our sin separated even the Son of God from intimate fellowship with the Father. Our failure and our shame drove spikes into His hands and feet. Your shame and mine cost Jesus His life. Yet the Scriptures proclaim, "He made Him who knew no sin to be sin on our behalf, so that we might become the righteousness of God in Him" (2 Corinthians 5:21).

In other words, He took our place on that *blest cross!* In that *blest sepulcher!* Let's face it, there are and there will be moments in our lives when we get "caught in the very act." It may not be adultery but something else. It's sin just the same. But because of Jesus we don't have to live a life of self-condemnation and debilitating shame. The Savior's words to you in your tough stuff of shame are the same now as they were then: "I do not condemn you either. Go. From now on sin no more." That means you're free.

If you're reading this and feeling the weight of your own shameful past or stubborn sinful ways, I invite you to come to the Savior. He's the only One perfectly qualified to judge you and condemn you, but because of what His death accomplished, He is ready to forgive and to set you free. His invitation to freedom requires your response. It isn't automatic. Being delivered from shame's shackles necessitates your coming to the precipice of the cross and acknowledging your need for Jesus. He will be there to cleanse you and make you whole.

Are you tired? Worn out? Burned out on religion? Come to me. Get away with me and you'll recover your life. I'll show you how to take a real rest. Walk with me and work with me—watch how I do it. Learn the unforced rhythms of grace. I won't lay anything heavy or ill-fitting on you. Keep company with me and you'll learn to live freely and lightly. (Matthew 11:28–30 MSG)

The "unforced rhythms of grace" will truly and completely set you free. So what are you waiting for?

Five

Getting Through the Tough Stuff of Doubt

DOUBT PROMPTS A BROAD RANGE OF OPINIONS. To a few, doubt represents rank unbelief, the worst kind of blasphemy. To others, doubt exposes more the raw side of honesty—that part of you never before seen until it's probed deeply with the penetrating questions of life. It boils down to this: Can we have lingering doubts and remain a person of faith? Strong and capable people on both sides disagree.

The great reformer, Martin Luther, had absolutely no place in his theology for doubt. He scored few things more scathingly than what he termed that "monster of uncertainty," a "gospel of despair."[1] But Alfred Lord Tennyson, on the other hand, wrote, "There lives more faith in honest doubt, Believe me, than in half the creeds."[2]

Down through the centuries the church has had representatives on both sides. On the one hand, there have always been the Jonathan

Edwardses, the George Whitefields, the Dwight L. Moodys, whose strong pulpits have rung with such assurance you would wonder as you read their sermons if they at any time ever entertained a doubt. On the other hand, God has given His church C. S. Lewis, Flannery O'Connor, Blaise Pascal, and more recently, Philip Yancey, who have encouraged us to question.

Is it possible for faith and doubt to coexist? One desperate parent in the New Testament would answer that question with a resounding, "Yes!" He's the father of the demon-possessed boy, who in anguish turned to Jesus for help. His had been a long, dark night attempting every imaginable remedy for his son's horrifying and torturous madness. Nothing worked. The scene that Mark's Gospel includes captures, like few others in the Bible, the very real conflict between hope and despair.

> They brought the boy to Him. When he saw Him, immediately the spirit threw him into a convulsion, and falling to the ground, he began rolling around and foaming at the mouth. And He asked his father, "How long has this been happening to him?" And he said, "From childhood. It has often thrown him both into the fire and into the water to destroy him. But if You can do anything, take pity on us and help us!" And Jesus said to him, "'If You can?' All things are possible to him who believes." Immediately the boy's father cried out and said, "I do believe; help my unbelief." (Mark 9:20–24)

WHEN DOUBTS EMERGE

The anguished father watching his son writhe on the ground like a rabid animal strained against the tough stuff of doubt to muster sufficient faith to believe. And he was bold enough to acknowledge it as well as request Jesus's help to overcome it. I'm so glad God decided to include that candid dialogue in Scripture, aren't you?

You may find yourself occupying a place in the ranks of the doubters of this world. If so, this chapter is written especially with you in mind. To exacerbate matters, you may live among people who have never once questioned their faith. Their piety makes you feel isolated, even a little weird . . . out of place. Perhaps your doubts have sunk you to the depth of despair. You too have cried, "Lord, I believe. Help me in my unbelief."

Daniel Taylor, in his book *The Myth of Certainty*, doesn't choose to use the term "doubting Christians." He refers to the doubters among us as "reflective Christians." Frankly, that works for me. There's not much dignity in doubt, but there is a touch of dignity in reflection. Taylor offers a variety of questions that represent the common struggles of a reflective Christian. Here's a sampling:

- Does one minute it seem perfectly natural and unquestionable that God exists and cares for the world, and the next moment uncommonly naive?

- Have you sometimes felt like walking out of a church service because it seemed contrived and empty?

- Someone at work says, "Christians check their brains at the door of the church every Sunday, and most of them don't even bother to pick them up on the way out." Do you find yourself objecting or agreeing?

- How confident are you that you know God's desires regarding the specific political, social, and moral issues which face our society?[3]

According to Daniel Taylor, a nonreflective person asks, "What could be worse than unanswered questions?" To him, the reflective person would consider *unquestioned answers* his or her struggle. A reflective Christian is one who is thinking deeply, questioning often. When we doubt, our minds are at work.

Taylor goes on to explain,

> There is a long tradition of people of faith who have valued and participated in the life of the mind and who have brought their God-given intelligence and imagination to bear on the society in which they have lived. These believers have been involved thoughtfully in their cultures, sometimes as shapers, sometimes as critics, but always as people who thought the human endeavor worthwhile.
>
> But there is also a more troublesome aspect to being reflective. Thinking, as many have discovered, can be dangerous. It can get us in trouble—with others, but also with ourselves. And the suspicion lingers in religious circles that it can also, if we are not very careful, get us in trouble with God.[4]

When are those times I allow my intellect to challenge my beliefs? When do I question? When do I reflect? And candidly, when do I doubt? Likely, it's at those same crossroads of doubt and faith common to most of us. When we encounter a sudden, unexpected calamity. When we pray for a specific outcome and the exact opposite occurs. When we lose a valued staff member or coworker or when our dearest friend moves away to another state. When we live right and suffer miserably for it. When we take a course at school that makes more sense than what our church believes. Ouch!

When life takes us through unexpected twists and tragic turns, we're often overwhelmed by the tough stuff of doubt.

Thankfully the Bible does not leave us awash in our questions. A familiar story in John's Gospel shows us that the answer to much of our doubting is a Person. His name is Jesus and—as He did for one struggling disciple—He helps us in our unbelief . . . transforming those lingering questions into more stabilized faith.

A REFLECTIVE THOMAS

Remember Doubting Thomas? Of course you do. Talk about a bad rap that stuck! My heart goes out to the poor guy. I'd rather think of him, thanks to Daniel Taylor's analysis, as *Reflective Thomas*. He's the one honest disciple who didn't check his brain at the synagogue door. He had faith in his doubts when his questions weren't answered. He had the guts to question the crowd, to raise his hand and press for answers that made better sense. I call that kind of honesty not only reassuring but valiant. I would love to see the ranks of Christianity filled with more courageous believers willing to declare openly the struggles they have, to weep when they're hurting, to admit their doubts rather than deny them.

In the Shadow of Certain Death

John 11 portrays a raw expression of doubt in the midst of life's tough stuff. Here we meet our man Thomas, his mind engaged and his faith again on the ropes.

Two days after hearing of Lazarus's death, Jesus announced to His disciples that He would be going up to Judea, where Lazarus would certainly be buried. The disciples knew the dangers of going back. Jesus was Public Enemy Number One on Judea's most-wanted list. To complicate things, the religious leaders were already breathing vicious threats against His life.

Not surprisingly, the Twelve attempted to dissuade Jesus from altering His itinerary and walking into harm's way. "Rabbi, the Jews were just now seeking to stone You, and are You going there again?" (v. 8).

I can't speak for you, but that response makes good sense to me.

Not persuaded, Jesus insisted on returning to Judea, saying, "Lazarus is dead, and I am glad for your sakes that I was not there, so that you may believe; but let us go to him" (vv. 14–15). At that point something remarkable happened. Reflective Thomas, the one haunted by doubts, spoke up. John writes, "Therefore Thomas . . . said to his fellow disciples, 'Let us also go, so that we may die with Him'" (v. 16).

A chill had no doubt run the length of Thomas's spine when he heard Jesus talk of going back to Bethany. But that chill was quickly transformed into iron resolve. He knew the danger and apparently resigned himself to the irreversible decision to follow Jesus, regardless . . . a decision which would eventually cost him his life.

Yet doubt lingers in Thomas's words. New Testament scholar Merrill Tenney writes, "His faith was courageous but not triumphant. He was resigned to the possibility of martyrdom as a matter of duty, but he did not entertain the concept of a victory over death and all its powers. Faith had not yet passed from resolution to insight."[5]

All Thomas could envision in the trip to Bethany was certain death. I call that reality. But he didn't know of anybody he'd rather die with than his Master and the other disciples. I call that loyalty.

In the Face of an Uncertain Future

John 14 shows that Thomas had his doubts about the future too. They had come to Jerusalem. It was there Jesus stood in the darkening shadow of the Cross. He slipped away to a second-story flat in the busy city where He and the Twelve would gather for their final meal. Jesus has broken the news to them that His death was near. Separation from them was certain. As He scanned the room for their reactions, He read fear and doubt in their eyes. That's when He spoke what are perhaps some of His most tender words as He attempted to calm their worried minds and steel their shaken resolve.

> Do not let your heart be troubled; believe in God, believe also in Me. In My Father's house are many dwelling places; if it were not so, I would have told you; for I go to prepare a place for you. If I go and prepare a place for you, I will come again and receive you to Myself, that where I am, there you may be also. And you know the way where I am going. (John 14:1–4)

Jesus hardly finished His words before Thomas blurted out, "Lord, we do not know where You are going, how do we know the way?" (v. 5). I love his unguarded honesty! The rest of the men were thinking the same thing, but only Thomas had the guts to say so. He wasn't arguing, and he wasn't trying to stop the plan. He was stating the truth. He didn't have a clue where Jesus would be going, so he questioned Jesus's comment, ". . . you know the way." The fact is he didn't. None of them knew. That's why he asks, "How do we know the way?"

"Jesus said to him, 'I am the way, and the truth, and the life; no one comes to the Father but through Me. If you had known Me, you would have known My Father also; from now on you know Him, and have seen Him'" (vv. 6–7).

Now think this through. Had Thomas not expressed his doubts in the form of that question, it's possible Jesus might have never uttered those remarkable words . . . words, in fact, that have brought both hope and comfort to the world since that day. So, good question, Thomas. Good for you.

In the midst of the tough stuff of doubting, Thomas was willing to say, "I don't have this theology wrapped up cleanly in my mind, Jesus. It isn't clear to me. There's something about this heaven talk I can't weave together in my thoughts." Without a hint of rebuke, Jesus graciously worked with Thomas and respected his doubts. He understood his confusion. His fear. His grief.

Truth be told, Thomas's heart was broken. His dreams shattered. His hopes dashed. His plan to hold stock in a triumphant earthly kingdom went belly-up in a single declaration of intent. Not long after that honest interchange between Jesus and His disciples, Thomas watched from a distance as Jesus endured a violent, torturous death. He saw the blood splatter on the road. He saw those thick, iron spikes disappear deep into Christ's hands and feet. He grimaced as the sword pierced His side. Suddenly everything was over. With that, Reflective Thomas went AWOL—vanishing into the shadows of that confusing, depressing day in Jerusalem . . . leaving the man devastated. He checked out.

Before we go much further, I need to acknowledge that reflective people usually suffer alone. People like Thomas gravitate toward times of solitude and seclusion. (I know . . . I'm one of them.)

Even the people close to me seldom know those issues I struggle with intensely. Perhaps they shouldn't. But the struggles are there. Now don't misunderstand. I don't doubt my faith in the Lord Jesus. I certainly don't doubt His blood that paid the complete price for my sins and His resurrection from the grave. But like Thomas, I have questions. Many of them. My book of learning hasn't been sealed and shipped. My thoughts are still on the presses and they're rolling. The ink's not dry on my journal of questions. I confess to you that it is not uncommon for me in a given week to struggle deeply with things that make me wrestle within and wonder.

When my father died at the age of eighty-seven, he had lived with us for four years before we found it necessary to admit him to a very fine, clean place where he lived a while longer. He was kept under the watchful care of my sister and me during his final days in the hospital. I grieved silently. Yet when it came to my duties as a pastor of a growing, dynamic church, it was like someone threw a switch and I pressed on in my responsibilities.

I preached Dad's funeral to a small gathering of family and friends. I spoke somberly and appropriately about the promises of God and the hope we have beyond the grave. I buried my father's frail body with grace and poise, as all good ministers do. I never missed a beat. I've done that duty hundreds of times throughout my many years in the ministry. I could do much of it with my eyes closed . . . but always with tenderness and compassion.

My sister, Luci, and I got back on the plane to return home. During a quiet moment she asked, "Babe, do you believe every single thing you said today?" It made me think . . . deeply.

"No," I said, almost sighing under my breath. "There are things that the jury's still out on in my mind."

"That's not what I'm asking," she said back to me gently. "I know you believe a lot of it. I just want to know if you fully believe *every single thing.* 'Cause if you do, we're very different."

I said, "No. There are things that I really have a hard time believing and understanding. I just can't fit everything together in my mind and in my heart." She paused, then lovingly put her hand on my arm and with tears in her eyes answered, "That's good, Babe. And that's okay." Perhaps softened by her tender expression of love and honesty, I looked at the clouds outside the window as tears began to flow for my dad and for our losing him.

I fear that too many believers think they have captured the message of Christianity and placed it in a box marked on top, "Don't ask. Don't tell." On the side it reads, "Off limits for doubts and questions."

Does someone in the family need to give you permission to weep when you lose a loved one? I mean, really grieve? Do you feel the freedom to admit, "I just don't know for sure?" Is there a place for you because you're still thinking and still questioning? Bottom line: Is it okay to doubt? It's okay! In fact, it is necessary! You must or you won't grow. You'll wind up learning someone else's answers, and in many cases they will be inadequate for your questions . . . if you're honest enough to ask them.

I find airtight conclusions mainly in people who have not hurt much. They're usually people who have become tightly wired, rigid, and isolated from the real world. They're closed . . . unwilling to be vulnerable. Suddenly, a divorce comes. Or someone dies in a tragic set of circumstances, or loses his job. Reality hits and a storm blows in and threatens their once tranquil existence. The emotional explosion results in more questions than answers. They discover things they didn't really know. They are in the vortex of dilemmas they cannot solve. At that point simplistic solutions are replaced with realistic reflections . . . and the deep things of God begin to emerge, eclipsing shallow answers.

That explains why Jesus doesn't rebuke Thomas and say, "Look in your notebook! We covered that in my discourse on the Mount of Olives—page 59." He said in effect, "Thomas, your questions will be settled in Me. I am the way and the truth and the life" (John 14:6).

How could He be "the Way" when they found themselves at a dead end? How could He call Himself "the Truth" when it all appears to have been a hoax? How could He have been "the Life" when they had just been told of His impending death? More unresolved questions lingered in Thomas's fractured soul. For three days after Christ's death, the disciples grieved, haunted by fear, dogged by doubt. Then, when Jesus appeared to them, all that changed.

John remembers the transforming encounter:

So when it was evening on that day, the first day of the week, and when the doors were shut where the disciples were, for fear of the Jews, Jesus came and stood in their midst and said to them, "Peace be with you." And when He had said this, He showed them both His hands and His side. The disciples then rejoiced when they saw the Lord. So Jesus said to them again, "Peace be with you; as the Father has sent Me, I also send you. . . ."

But Thomas, one of the twelve, called Didymus, was not with them when Jesus came. (John 20:19–21, 24)

With hopes dashed and dreams gone, Thomas was nowhere to be found. He was lost in his doubts and disillusionment. Wherever he was, though, the remaining disciples soon found him and exclaimed, "We have seen the Lord!"

But that was not enough for our reflective friend. He wanted tangible proof. That's why Thomas said to them, "Unless I see in His hands the imprint of the nails, and put my finger into the place of the nails, and put my hand into His side, I will not believe" (v. 25).

Once again Thomas owned his doubts. He did not blindly believe because others did. It would take more than a few excited friends to convince him that the horrible events he had witnessed only days before were somehow miraculously reversed. He wanted to touch Jesus's hands, feel the deep imprint of the nail scars, and put his finger in the spear wound in His side before he could come around. And that is just what Jesus had in mind for Thomas. John writes of that event too:

After eight days His disciples were inside, and Thomas with them. Jesus came, the doors having been shut, and stood in their midst and said, "Peace be with you." Then He said to Thomas, "Reach here with your finger, and see My hands; and reach here your hand and put it into My side; and do not be unbelieving, but believing." Thomas answered and said to Him, "My Lord and my God!" (vv. 26–28)

Thomas, having honestly faced his doubts, discovered a firm faith. Once convinced, he yielded.

We get through the tough stuff of doubt the same way—by facing those doubts and bringing them to the Savior! Just like Thomas.

Any question asked without guile is not a skeptical question. It's an honest search. Jesus very graciously responds, "Because you have seen Me, have you believed? Blessed are they who did not see, and yet believed" (v. 29).

You're in the "they" of that sentence. "Blessed are you who did not see, and yet believe." Blessed are you, Mary, Doris, Barbara, and Martha. Blessed are you, Bob, Bill, Nathan, and Frank. Blessed are all who haven't seen, yet believe! Blessed are you for bringing your doubts to Him and leaving them at the foot of the cross. It is there— at the cross—where those who can no longer cope with life's doubts are able to work things through. It is the place to which we all must come . . . sooner rather than later.

When You Cannot Cope

May I close this chapter by writing very personally to you? Yes, you. Throughout any life that is lived realistically and reflectively, we come to impossible places where we feel we cannot cope. They may not seem like it, but those are the healthiest places in life, but they are also the hardest. When the bottom drops out, when the pain seems unbearable, when some unbelievable event occurs, doubts arrive unannounced. Don't deny them; acknowledge them. Those times of doubting become schoolrooms of learning. As we work our way through them, a new kind of faith is forged. It will come slowly, and that's healthy. It's being shaped on the anvil of God's mysterious plan, some of which you will not be able to explain. And that's okay.

Now the real question is how. How do we grow this new kind of faith in the tough stuff of doubt?

First, by risking and failing, not always playing it safe. You can't afford to live a life of fear. You must not always play life safe. Winning over doubts means beginning to live by faith and not by sight. Walking this new journey has its risks. You cannot see around every bend or anticipate every danger. You will sometimes fail, but that isn't fatal! That's how we grow, by trusting God through the risks we take and the failures we endure. Step out. Refuse to play it safe.

Second, we keep growing by releasing and losing things valuable, not finding security in the temporal. At the heart of this technique is the principle of holding all things loosely.

Cynthia and I know a couple who have to be as close to the ideal set of parents as we've ever met. Every Christmas we get a lovely card from them. For years they were to us the picture-perfect family. Yet one day they found themselves in an inescapable abyss. Their precious daughter was admitted to a psychiatric facility after attempting suicide over an eating disorder. Our dear friends hit absolute bottom. They weren't grinning and quoting verses. They didn't run around smiling at life, quoting tired clichés, like, "In spite of this, God is great, God is good." No, they nearly drowned in their doubts. They wept bitter tears. They questioned everything they ever believed.

Are they still qualified as people of faith though they wavered in the dark? Absolutely. By God's grace, in time, they released those doubts, having faced them honestly, and they refused to seek security in the temporal. Today, looking back, they're convinced those lonely days proved to be some of the best days of their lives. Their walk with the Lord is far more mature than before.

Third, we continue to grow by questioning and probing the uncertain, not mindlessly embracing the orthodox. Read that once again, aloud. We don't just blindly swallow someone else's answers. We keep our minds and our hearts engaged in the pursuit of God's truth. By searching the Scriptures. By seeking God's wisdom and understanding. That's what I mean by questioning and probing.

Fourth, we grow by admitting and struggling with our humanity, not denying our limitations and hiding our fears. And I can assure you that this author for God understands when you find yourself cornered by doubt. I've been there more times than you'd ever believe. You are definitely not alone.

Don't Doubt, Believe

Perhaps you have just read for the first time in your life that there is room at the Cross for your doubts and your questions. Maybe some well-meaning soul has pushed you into a corner and attempted to make you believe or tried to force you into feeling your questions are an offense to Christ. You need to hear anew the tender words of One who knows your doubts and fears better than you. He says, "Peace be with you. Look at My hands and feet. Look with eyes of faith and believe. You are blessed when you believe in spite of your doubts."

⁓

Lord, our faith has found a resting place in Your Son, Jesus. Still, like Thomas, we struggle with fears—we entertain doubts. We haven't put life all together yet. Not until we're with You will that happen. Thank You for accepting us in our struggles, and thank You for not ignoring our questions. We have asked some of them a hundred times it seems. Thank You for understanding that, though we weep over our losses, we still love You. And when we question the tragedies and calamities of life, it isn't that we doubt Your right to rule . . . we're wrestling to release our own rights. We're trying to reason our way through.

Thank You for not rejecting us when we fail. Thank You for not leaving us to our doubts. Thank You for the message of Your Book, which includes honest folks like Thomas, who finally did say, "My Lord and my God." Have patience with us as we try to come to that place too.

I pray this in Jesus's name. Amen.

Six

Getting Through the Tough Stuff of Divorce

I'M A PREACHER. That's my gift and my passion. Whether I'm doing research in the quietness of my study or speaking in a place of worship surrounded by people, what flows from the depth of my being are sermons—observations and implications, applications and exhortations from God's Word. All these have passed through the grid of my soul, pressed through my fingers onto the page, and finally expressed from my lips, first to my congregation and finally across the airwaves.

All sermons, whether written or spoken, must be instructive in nature. They must be based on the truth of God, not human opinion. Nearly a century ago another preacher, far more gifted than I, Charles Haddon Spurgeon, spoke the following words to his students as he urged them to go hard after truth and substantive doctrine in their preaching:

SERMONS *should have real teaching in them,* and their doctrine should be solid, substantial, and abundant. We do not enter the pulpit to talk for talk's sake; we have instructions to convey, important to the last degree, and we cannot afford to utter pretty nothings. Our range of subjects is all but boundless, and we cannot, therefore, be excused if our discourses are threadbare and devoid of substance.[1]

As I planned my approach to this chapter on the harsh realities of divorce, I deliberately resisted the temptation to write "pretty nothings." There's nothing pretty about divorce. You know that, if you've been through the trauma, or know someone who has. We need God's perspective—His unadulterated truth from the pages of His Word coupled with the tender, clear expressions of His Son, Jesus.

I confess, as I write this chapter, I do so with a heavy heart. This is a sad and sober subject. But since divorce is so common in our day, a book about getting through the tough stuff of life would have been dismally abridged without a chapter on the topic. Hopefully, once you've interacted with the teaching of Scripture, you will be challenged to deeper thinking and more careful living.

More than that, if you're at the crossroad of divorce or struggling with thoughts of leaving your mate, you need to know you are not alone. The One who understands your deepest longing and most private burdens cares about your pain and can identify with your disappointment. His name is Jesus. He knows all the reasons you feel you'd be better off walking away from your marriage. Still, He stands alongside you today, not ready to wag His divine finger and scold you for your lack of faith, but anxious to calm and comfort you, help you think even deeper, and bring a fresh resolve to trust Him for another day.

So, will you hang in there with me for the next several pages? If you're in the middle of a brutal divorce or looking for a way of escape from a broken and painful relationship, these may not be easy truths to read and ponder. But stay with me, please. By listening to God as

He speaks through His Word, I can offer you reliable counsel from Him who is the Wonderful Counselor and the Prince of Peace. Stop and remember, He originated the whole idea of marriage. He's the marriage Designer, the supreme Architect. He's the best-qualified counselor to help you in your broken relationship. He's the One who created you in the first place.

So the first stop in our journey for perspective is a trip back in time. Let's return to the biblical blueprints for marriage to see how it all got started.

WHEN MARRIAGE BEGAN

Marriage began shortly after the beginning of human life. The very first chapter of Genesis provides a sweeping statement of God's activity in the first six days of creation. The climax of His creation of the earth and the entire universe comes when God says, "Let Us make man in Our image, according to Our likeness; and let them rule over the fish of the sea and over the birds of the sky and over the cattle and over all the earth, and over every creeping thing that creeps on the earth" (Genesis 1:26). The inspired narrator continues, "God created man in His own image, in the image of God He created him; male and female He created them" (v. 27).

Genesis 2 moves like a zoom lens under the direction of the Holy Spirit and chronicles the sequence of mankind's creation. First we read of the creation of Adam: "Then the LORD God formed man of dust from the ground, and breathed into his nostrils the breath of life; and man became a living being" (v. 7).

Next, God created a woman:

Then the LORD God said, "It is not good for the man to be alone; I will make him a helper suitable for him." . . . So the

LORD God caused a deep sleep to fall upon the man, and he slept; then He took one of his ribs and closed up the flesh at that place. The LORD God fashioned into a woman the rib which He had taken from the man, and brought her to the man. (vv. 18, 21–22)

That must have been a magnificent scene. Talk about a beautiful wedding! Seeing the loneliness and barrenness of Adam's soul, God decided to step in and change all that. Amazingly, from Adam's rib He fashioned a unique, lovely, living being—a woman. And God brought Eve to Adam in the first-ever marriage relationship. No wedding march, no bridal gown, no ring ceremony, no sweaty palms, no stressed-out wedding planner barking orders at the ushers. Only a peaceful garden scene with God, a man, and a woman coming together. Perfect. Perfect harmony. Perfect match. Perfect plan . . . spelled out in the simplest of terms: "For this reason a man shall leave his father and his mother, and be joined to his wife; and they shall become one flesh. And the man and his wife were both naked and were not ashamed" (vv. 24–25).

In that brief narrative God imbeds His original blueprint for the ideal marriage plan:

- The first marriage was between a man and a woman.

- The couple was brought together by God Himself.

- They were to live out their relationship God's way and for God's glory.

A careful look at the plan reveals four essential ingredients: *severance, permanence, unity,* and *intimacy.* Let's consider each one.

First, there must be severance. "A man shall leave his father and mother." The kind of marriage God originally planned requires that both bride and groom break dependent ties with original parents or guardians. That ensures that the marriage relationship begins with no competing emotions. It also implies a clear dependence on God and interdependence on each other.

Second, there must be permanence. "And shall be joined to his wife." The word translated "be joined to" literally means "to bond or to glue." There is permanence in mind. Adam and Eve were to have an impenetrable and lasting relationship.

The third essential is unity. "And they shall become one flesh." That's not uniformity. The man and woman were to remain distinct. They were to enjoy different roles. They were to maintain their unique, God-given traits and temperaments. Those uniquenesses notwithstanding, God planned an overarching unity that is to prevail—a lifelong cultivation of a unified relationship.

Appropriately, the final touch God planned is intimacy. "The man and his wife were both naked and were not ashamed." In Adam and Eve's case, this was a tender, God-ordained intimacy untarnished by sin. Unfettered by shame. Absent of self-consciousness. The intimate emotional freedom and sexual delights of that first husband and wife were beyond our comprehension. Their marriage was perfect. Absolutely perfect . . . until Genesis 3.

WHERE MARRIAGE WENT WRONG

What went wrong? The answer in a word: *sin.* You likely know the story. God allowed Adam and Eve perfect freedom to live in and enjoy the fruitfulness of the garden. He gave only one prohibition: they were not to eat the fruit of the tree of the knowledge of good and evil. To do so would bring both spiritual and physical death (Genesis 2:17). But they didn't obey God. Eating the forbidden fruit, they set in motion an avalanche of destruction and evil.

Sin took its toll on *permanence,* perhaps more so than *severance* and *unity* and *intimacy.* Sin weakened the marriage bond sealed at God's holy altar. Rather than preach here, I'll simply cut to the chase. If there is one massive blot on the record of human relationships since that day until now, it would be the breakdown of permanence in marriage.

What Happened to Permanence?

Statistics reveal an epidemic. If the trend continues, more than half of all American marriages will end in divorce in their first decade. Though that disturbs me, there are two sides of this that greatly trouble me. It pains me even to mention them here, but I must.

First, I'm troubled by the fact that Christian couples are as susceptible to divorce as are non-Christians. In spite of the inexhaustible divine resources at our disposal, the odds of a Christian marriage lasting a lifetime are just as low as for unbelievers. Followers of Jesus Christ are choosing to walk away from their marriage commitments in alarming numbers that increase every year.

The second part that bothers me so much is the havoc divorce brings to children. And that devastation includes adult children of divorce. Today, less than three-quarters of all American children live in two-parent homes. And the scene isn't much better in many other countries. Divorce is crippling the emerging generations.

Why Be So Concerned?

What's the big deal? you may wonder. Put bluntly, because divorce is not as God planned it, nor does it please Him. Divorce in the church is nothing short of an epidemic. Plain and simple, God planned that there be one man with one woman in a marriage that lasts for a lifetime. God is pleased when two parents of the opposite sex rear their children in a healthy fear and tender instruction of the Lord. God is honored and wonderfully pleased when families function with open communication, role modeling, confidence building, love, discipline, safety and security (to name only a few). In fact, God wants His church to model those distinctives—not to blur them with divorce.

Another critical concern is that divorce starts a cycle that never improves—it always erodes. Once the thought of getting out of a marriage becomes an option, the permanence of marriage is subtly undermined. And once that mentality takes over, the slippery slope picks up speed. History tells the sad tale that once a nation's homes are permanently fractured, the nation will crumble at its foundation.

We who have spent our lives in a context of pervasive sin cannot imagine what life would be like in a world of pervasive innocence. Just stop and think. Make two columns in your mind.

Innocence	Sinfulness
Peace, harmony, and joy Open communication, intimacy, desire to obey God	Conflict, strife, and hatred Closed communication, selfishness, a desire to please me, or to blame you if you don't make me happy, or blame God if He doesn't bring it to pass
Love, affection, care, security, and sacrificial commitment	Demands, anger, competition, low self-esteem

Writer John Powell does a masterful job in his book *Happiness is an Inside Job* of describing how we naively hope for happiness in the life of another person. Read his words carefully and thoughtfully.

A few years ago a divorce lawyer submitted the opinion that most divorces result from romanticized expectations. Jack thinks that being married to Jill will be utter bliss. He calls her "Angel" and "Sweetie." She is all he will ever need. He sings her the romantic lyrics of love songs. Then, shortly after the wedding bells have become an echo, the truth sets in: There are unpleasant moods, weight gains, burned dinners, hair curlers, occasional bad breath and body odors. He silently wonders how he ever got into this. He secretly thinks she has deceived him. He had gambled his happiness on "Angel Face" and has apparently lost.

On the other side, before marriage Jill's heart beats a little faster whenever she thinks of Jack. It will be such heaven to be married to him. "Just Jackie and me and baby makes three . . . in my Blue Heaven." Then there are cigarette ashes, his addiction to sports events on television, minor but painful insensitivities. Clothes are left lying only in chronological order. Her knight in shining armor has turned out to be a "one-man slum." The top of the toothpaste tube is missing. The doorknob he promised to fix still comes off in her hand. Jill cries a lot, starts looking up "marriage counselors" in the yellow pages. Jack carried her off gallantly into the sunset. From then on it was all darkness.

Fifty percent of all marriages end in divorce. Sixty-five percent of all second marriages end in the same traumatic sadness. Disillusion always seems to follow when we expect someone or something else to make us happy. Such expectations are a parade that always gets rained on. The place called "Camelot" and the person called "Right" just don't exist. . . . I once saw a cartoon of a huge woman standing over her diminutive, seated husband, demanding, "Make me happy!" It was a cartoon. It was meant for laughter. It was a distortion of reality. And that's why it was funny. No one can make us truly happy or truly unhappy.[2]

When will we learn that? Marriage was never designed to make you or anyone else happy. Therefore your unhappiness is no reason to end a lifetime of commitment. Happiness is icing on the cake. As I have said for years, it is not love that keeps a marriage together; it is commitment. Love, as an emotion, ebbs and flows over time. There are only so many moonlit nights to go around. Sickness, heartache, brokenness, disease, aging, and adversity all work against romantic love, but those same struggles are able to strengthen commitment.

All of this bad news underscores the destructive power of sin. Since the mudslide of sin began in Genesis 3, all marriages have strained against sin's wrecking influence. Strife, abuse, deception, low self-esteem, selfishness, and immorality—throw all those into the marriage mix, and there's no wonder we need God's power to survive. The good news is this: There is hope in Christ for getting through the tough stuff of divorce, no matter where you find yourself in the cycle.

In Jesus's Day: His Instruction on Divorce

The base camp of Christ's teaching on divorce is found in Matthew 19. Jesus was concerned about divorce even in His day, since it was particularly rampant both among the common people as well as the Pharisees. Matthew captures a scene in chapter 19 of his Gospel that shows the religious leaders once again attempting to trap Jesus, but this time the trap was set around the issue of divorce.

"Some Pharisees came to Jesus, testing Him and asking, 'Is it lawful for a man to divorce his wife for any reason at all?'" (v. 3).

To understand what prompted the Pharisees' question, we must first understand an event that occurred in the history of the Hebrew people. In the beginning, God intended that Israel be His witness to the rest of the world. But the ancient Jewish people, struggling in unbelief, finally caved in to worldly patterns of selfish living. That led them to intermarry with neighboring Gentiles. The *distinctiveness* between Jew and Gentile became increasingly more blurred. In order to correct their error and preserve the purity of the nation, God permitted Moses to release a certificate of divorce if "some indecency" was found in the marriage partner (see Deuteronomy 24:1–4). This was to be the exception, however, never the rule. As John Stott points out, divorce was "only a divine concession to human weakness."[3]

Various Answers

Admittedly there are a variety of interpretations of the meaning of "some indecency." That phrase would sharply divide the people of Jesus's day. Biblical scholar D. A. Carson writes,

> Opinion was divided roughly into two opposing camps: both the school of Hillel and the school of Shammai permitted divorce (of the woman by the man: the reverse was not considered) on the grounds of *erwat dabar* ("something indecent," Deuteronomy 24:1), but they disagreed on what "indecent" might include. Shammai and his followers interpreted the expression to refer to gross indecency, though not necessarily adultery; Hillel extended the meaning beyond sin to all kinds of

real or imagined offenses, including an improperly cooked meal. Hillelite R. Akiba permitted divorce in case of a roving eye for prettier women.[4]

The Pharisees hoped to draw Jesus straight into the Hillel versus Shammai controversy where they could ambush Him either way He answered. Jesus saw through their strategy, and rather than being pulled into the fray, He proceeded to align Himself with the prophet Malachi, who recorded God's own words on the matter when he wrote, "I hate divorce" (Malachi 2:16). Regardless of cultural acceptance, divorce is not normal, nor is it neutral, nor is it a pious promise of an easy way out of conflict. Divorce has always been destructive. Its consequences have always been far-reaching and long-lasting. Though sometimes, admittedly, it is permitted.

A Careful Analysis

Jesus chose to focus the Pharisees' attention on God's original design for marriage when He replied, "Have you not read that He who created them from the beginning made them male and female and said, 'For this reason a man shall leave his father and mother and be joined to his wife, and the two shall become one flesh'?" (Matthew 19:4–5). He then drove home the permanence and sanctity of marriage with a powerful command: "What therefore God has joined together, let no man separate" (v. 6).

The Pharisees persisted by probing further, "Why then did Moses command to give her a certificate of divorce and send her away?" (v. 7). Jesus didn't even blink. In His answer to that follow-up question He offered three critical clarifications, two of which are found in verse 8. Jesus replied, "Because of your hardness of heart Moses permitted you to divorce your wives; but from the beginning it has not been this way" (v. 8). Jesus first corrected the Pharisees: Moses didn't *command* divorce, he *permitted* it. Second, Jesus reiterated that divorce was not in God's original plan when He said, "But from the beginning it has not been this way." Finally, Jesus specified the meaning of "some indecency"—the controversial passage from Deuteronomy 24:1, which fueled the debate that kept the Hillel and Shammai camps so sharply divided: "And I say to you, whoever divorces his wife, except for immorality, and marries another woman commits adultery" (v. 9).

The Greek term Matthew uses, translated "immorality," is *porneia*. We get our English word *pornography* from that original term. It is not limited to adultery, though it includes that. It could refer to incest, lesbian sex, homosexual acts, and most definitely a sustained lifestyle of sexual misconduct outside the marriage bond.

It seems doubtful that Jesus was giving permission for couples to divorce over a one-night stand. That's not the force of *porneia*. Using this word, Jesus emphasized a continued willingness on the part of the marriage partner to remain sexually unfaithful, to carry out an obvious determination to seek sexual intimacy with another individual outside of the marriage.

And let me add that the faithful partner is never *commanded* to leave. God (who hates divorce) desires that the faithful partner stay long enough to allow God the opportunity for the fractured marriage to work, to heal, to restore. I should also state that it can get fuzzy as to who's faithful and who's not. But the one who has *not* committed the series of indecent acts is encouraged to remain faithful and to allow God to work. I've watched people like that who later say, "Staying together was the best thing we ever did. I decided to forgive him. I understood that it was a failure, a breaking of our intimacy. And I don't know that we'll ever fully get past this point.

But I've determined that the children, the marriage, and our future are worth going on beyond this." You've heard of tough love. I call that response rugged commitment. I applaud it.

A Necessary Acceptance

Matthew never mentions if the Pharisees grasped the seriousness of Christ's teaching, but he gives us a hint that the disciples got it: "The disciples said to Him, 'If the relationship of the man with his wife is like this, it is better not to marry'" (Matthew 19:10).

Jesus affirms them and corrects them at the same time:

> But Jesus said, "Not everyone is mature enough to live a married life. It requires a certain aptitude and grace. Marriage isn't for everyone. Some, from birth seemingly, never give marriage a thought. Others never get asked—or accepted. And some decide not to get married for kingdom reasons. But if you're capable of growing into the largeness of marriage, do it." (Matthew 19:11–12 MSG)

In other words, if you have the gift of celibacy or are celibate for whatever reason, stay single . . . that's great! That's wonderful—accept your singleness as a gift from God. But if you choose to marry, take that commitment very seriously and make it permanent. That's God's original design and plan for marriage.

SOME HARD CONCLUSIONS THAT DEMAND A RESPONSE

Let me offer you three important thoughts to remember as you ponder Christ's teaching on divorce.

First, the sanctity of marriage necessitates personal commitment, just as the sanctity of life necessitates birth. We wouldn't dream of taking a life from the womb. That's abortion! And we would stand to the end against that. With equal passion we need to agree that the sanctity of marriage necessitates commitment. You have no right to abort your marriage simply because of its struggles, difficulties, or inconveniences. And I repeat, no marriage is held together simply by romantic love. Love is important. In fact, love is vital, but it can become thin and fragile over time. Commitment adds needed muscle when love suffers the fallout of fatigue.

Second, the necessity of commitment is weakened by our sinful nature. That's why in weak moments all of us are tempted to walk out. Sin enters, and with it comes compromise, a softening of our wills, and any number of byproducts of carnality: abuse, infidelity, selfishness, arguments, grudges held by one another, caustic remarks, embarrassment, sarcasm, and an endless number of other destructive tendencies. All that weakens the commitment. Without help at that point, some will not go on. You may be at that point as you are reading these thoughts very carefully.

Third, our sinful nature can be counteracted by Jesus Christ. He truly is the answer. He's the remedy, no matter how desperately dysfunctional your marriage has become. Without Him, we're all up the creek without a paddle. Frankly, I am amazed that any unbeliever can have a happy, fulfilled marriage. But you know what? Some can pull it off. I've seen what appear to be fulfilling and mutually gratifying marriages among non-Christians. Remarkably, they do it without any power from Christ. But their relationship never reaches the full heights the original Architect designed for marriage.

Without Jesus, a solid marriage is virtually impossible to maintain. And if your marriage is already on the rocks, you must not attempt to go through the tough stuff of even contemplating divorce without leaning hard on Jesus for His power. With Jesus at the core of both partners, no marriage is too far gone. There's never a point of no return if both are willing to surrender to Him and allow Him to work His way and in His time.

I had a young man say to me recently, "I want you to know that I have come back to my wife. We had separated and I quickly fell into an affair. I've suffered both the consequences and the futility of that. I'm telling you, I'm coming back. Chuck, I've never felt the sense of God's presence and strength as I do now."

That's what you need in the tough circumstances of a pending divorce or a troubled marriage: Christ's presence and strength. But, just to set the record straight, I need to say that He won't storm the citadel of your heart uninvited. He waits to come in—to be asked to work on your behalf or on behalf of your mate. To begin a supernatural work of healing and restoration, to reverse the years of pain, misunderstanding, bitterness, and haunting regret, Christ must be invited in.

Perhaps you've only recently experienced the horrors of a long, brutal divorce. You were left by your mate for another, more attractive individual. You're feeling discarded, used, and betrayed. You need to know that although I wish I could say I understand the depth of your pain, I really don't. I can't, since I've never experienced such abject rejection from the one I thought loved me more than anything in the world. But I know One who *can* understand. One who knows the sting and shame of rejection, the horror of injustice, and the shock of unfaithfulness. His name is Jesus. He endured all of that and so much more. So I point you to Him and to His blessed cross. Only He can take the shattered remains of your life and lovingly begin to put back the pieces, tenderly holding each one with compassionate care and empathy.

Perhaps for you it has been several years since your marriage ended in divorce. Yet the hurt lingers, especially in those times when you're most alone. Again, let me remind you: Jesus is there in those tough stretches of loneliness and shame that remain long after everyone else has moved on with their lives. Will you let Him comfort you today? I hope you will. Don't try to get through the tough stuff alone any longer, my friend. Trust Him completely, regardless of what you face. Refuse to give up. Let Him become your stability and strength. He waits for you to call on Him.

This has been straight talk, not "pretty nothings." But it's straight talk that's needed when the temptation to walk out is so strong. Unless it is absolutely essential for your survival, don't go there!

Seven

Getting Through the Tough Stuff of Remarriage

WHEN CYNTHIA AND I lived in Southern California, Mr. and Mrs. Mallard Duck flew into our backyard one cool afternoon. They had chosen our yard and swimming pool as their place of temporary abode. And from what I observed, they might have been on their honeymoon. It was a beautiful sight to behold as they often snuggled close and nuzzled each other.

The emerald green head of the male stayed close to his beloved mate in her soft-and-fluffy brown beauty. She sort of wiggled and quacked and coddled in enjoyment.

While lost in the beauty of it from our kitchen, I suddenly looked to my right and had to chuckle. Our big white dog Sha-sha (Russian Semoid) was trying to look like a pointer. She had focused in on one of the ducks. There I stood enjoying the delightful scene of two ducks feeling safe and romantic, while our dog was standing nearby, licking her chops, thinking about supper!

A nearly perfect analogy for marriage. First of all, I thought of the lovely bride and groom as they come to an altar reveling in the beauty and excitement of that special day—the lovely bride in exquisite white, the groom looking elegant in a black tuxedo and a bow tie. Both have that "thrilled look."

Sadly, though, many don't pay any attention to the dangers. They don't live happily ever after. As time passes, they neglect things of utmost importance and become preoccupied with lesser matters. They forget the predators that are lurking nearby.

Ducks are very devoted to one another. In fact, studies have documented that some even choose to die at the side of a mate shot out of the sky by a hunter. I find that fascinating.

Marriage was meant to be like that. Not an easy street, not a simple, happy-go-lucky lifestyle, but an exhilarating, wild, and dangerous frontier. Mike Mason, in an excellent work entitled *The Mystery of Marriage*, writes insightfully:

> Everywhere else, throughout society, there are fences, walls, burglar alarms, unlisted numbers, the most elaborate precautions for keeping people at a safe distance. But in marriage all of that is reversed. In marriage the walls are down, and not only do the man and woman live under the same roof, but they sleep under the same covers. Their lives are wide open, and as each studies the life of the other and attempts to make some response to it, there are no set procedures to follow, no formalities to stand on. A man and a woman face each other across the breakfast table, and somehow through a haze of crumbs and curlers and mortgage payments they must encounter one another. That is the whole purpose and mandate of marriage. All sorts of other purposes have been dreamed up and millions of excuses invented for avoiding this

central and indispensable task. But the fact is that marriage is grounded in nothing else but the pure wild grappling of soul with soul, no holds barred. There is no rulebook for this, no law to invoke, except the law of love.

So while marriage may present the appearance of being a highly structured, formalized, and tradition-bound institution, in fact it is the most free and raw and unpredictable of all human associations. It is the outer space of society, the wild frontier.[1]

And so it should be. Husbands and wives were meant to be those who fly free. Free alongside each other, partners bound together for life, who know the joys and ecstasies of intimacy, and who are willing to circle and stay near when the other falls, to stay alongside our chosen one to the very end. Too often we don't. And herein the allegory breaks down. The duck stays because it's a duck. Because of instinct. Just as it must fly north in the summer and south in the winter. But we are free not to stay. Divorce happens . . . all the time. Dangers appear. Relationships fracture. Commitment weakens. Predators pounce. Not surprisingly, the bond of love and permanence breaks. We saw the gravity of that in the previous chapter.

Time passes. As there are moments of neglect and forgetfulness when ducks fly too low, in range of men with big powerful guns, married couples can become negligent. They forget the predators that are well within range, always ready to make their moves.

Obviously anyone who views marriage as an endless ecstasy of romantic bliss, a sort of heaven on earth, is living in a dream world. I can testify, after almost fifty years with the same lady, it is the most challenging responsibility in life! Keeping our marriage strong, wholesome, fulfilling, and enriching is neither simple nor easy.

So rather than asking, "What are the grounds for divorce?" I would suggest that we give our attention to God's perspective on the tough stuff of remarriage. Here is a better question: When is remarriage acceptable in God's sight?

After a great deal of thought and time spent in my study, I have finally concluded that there are three situations set forth in the Bible where God allows remarriage. Let's take a look at each one.

SCRIPTURAL SURVEY OF REMARRIAGE SCENARIOS

In my view the Scriptures make plain these three situations. I want to review them here and then conclude this chapter with some sober warnings (*exhortations* may be a better word) to all who have made their commitment to marriage or who soon will.

Remarriage is permitted in the case of an unrepentant, immoral partner. In the previous chapter we looked at this first situation in a fair amount of detail; so we need only review it here. As you'll recall, the Pharisees determined to trap Jesus on the issue of divorce. His answer set them straight on several points.

> He said to them, "Because of the hardness of your heart Moses permitted you to divorce your wives; but from the beginning it has not been this way. And I say to you, whoever divorces his wife, except for immorality, and marries another woman commits adultery." (Matthew 19:8–9)

As we established earlier, the Lord hates divorce. But according to this passage there is something He hates just as much: to see the marriage bond stained and broken by spouses who continually pursue unholy lifestyles and who demonstrate a stubborn unwillingness to repent. In proof of how deeply He despises unfaithfulness,

Jesus permits the faithful spouse to divorce and eventually remarry.

Now don't misunderstand. I'm all for repentance. More importantly, so is the Lord. Divorce in such cases of stubborn rebellion and sustained immorality and a subsequent remarriage remain only a last resort. Almost without exception (and I really mean *almost without exception*), my counsel to people who come to me about such difficulties is, "Stay together and fully repent—fully forgive and try to make it work with God's help and the help of His people." And I will look into the face of the guilty, if he or she will admit the immorality, and plead for repentance, trying my best to bring about a change (I have literally begged for that!). But if that does not happen, I believe the exception clause in Matthew 19 permits the faithful partner, who has not committed any act of unfaithfulness, the option to walk away and to remarry. That is what Jesus states, and therefore that's what I believe. Again, I remind you, there are those who teach otherwise, and I respect them. I may disagree with them, but I respect their right to hold another position. What you will read in the pages that follow are the convictions I hold after more than four decades of scriptural study and pastoral practice.

Remarriage is permitted in the case of desertion by an unbelieving mate. Many single parents who love Christ could display in their Bibles a well-marked passage of Scripture. That passage is where we find the second situation in which God allows a victimized spouse to remarry following a failed marriage. All of us should be good students of the Scriptures, but those with threatened marriages should become serious and careful students of 1 Corinthians 7. If you're not, make a commitment to set aside a period of time to study this very helpful and insightful chapter.

Let me begin our consideration of this passage by describing the larger context. In the beginning verses of chapter 7, the apostle Paul reveals that if he had his "druthers," he would prefer that all people remain unmarried in order to dedicate their lives fully to Christ. He admits though that "each man has his own gift from God, one in this manner, and another in that" (v. 7). Those individuals who do not have the gift of celibacy—the God-given ability to remain single and content—are encouraged to pursue a marriage partnership with a member of the opposite sex.

In the balance of the chapter Paul describes three categories of people and how each group should approach the issue of marriage and remarriage. The first group he addresses is the group he refers to as "the unmarried" in verses 8–9. These are the unmarried and the widows. He prefers that they too remain unmarried, but if they simply cannot remain unmarried and content, they should marry or remarry, whichever the case.

Next, Paul addresses "the married," and to them he issues a challenge to *remain married.* More specifically he states that "the wife should not leave her husband (but if she does leave, she must remain unmarried, or else be reconciled to her husband), and that the husband should not divorce his wife" (vv. 10–11). He urged those already married to find contentment. Wives, make a study of your husband. Husbands, pursue your wives. Cultivate, relate, forgive, work together, and review those vows you took. Go back to where you started and repeat the courtship romances. Take time off during the weekends. Spend time deepening and harmonizing your relationship—whatever it takes, do it.

Consistently throughout his letters to believers, Paul advocated permanence in marriage. But he also understood harsher realities. Who knows why . . . or how? Perhaps he experienced a divorce in his own family somewhere down the line and felt empathy toward those individuals who simply could not be reconciled, and so he provides a temporary way of relief. To them he offered a parenthetical statement, allowing for separation until there could be genuine reconciliation. There are times, frankly, when an abused wife (or husband) must flee to preserve her or his own life or to protect the children. In desperate situations, separation is permitted for the sake of health and safety, with the understanding, I might add, that help would be sought and professional intervention pursued.

Finally, Paul addresses those who are "unequally yoked" in marriage—where a believer is married to an unbeliever—in verses 12–16. Carefully examine these penetrating, pastoral words. Read them slowly, several times. Think them through.

> But to the rest I say, not the Lord, that if any brother has a wife who is an unbeliever, and she consents to live with him, he must not divorce her. And a woman who has an unbelieving husband, and he consents to live with her, she must not send her husband away. For the unbelieving husband is sanctified through his wife, and the unbelieving wife is sanctified through her believing husband; for otherwise your children are unclean, but now they are holy. Yet if the unbelieving one leaves, let him leave; the brother or the sister is not under bondage in such cases, but God has called us to peace. For how do you know, O wife, whether you will save your husband? Or how do you know, O husband, whether you will save your wife? (1 Corinthians 7:12–16)

I find that great counsel for our day, don't you? Paul is urging for permanence where possible, even in a spiritually unbalanced relationship. The presence of a saved partner in the home sets the home apart, prompting God's blessings. The children are under the influence of biblical truth. At least one parent has been born again and knows the Lord personally. All the while, the mate who may not even care about the things of Christ lives his or her life in the presence of a saved, caring, compassionate, and loving partner. And in that sense, he or she is set apart for the things of Christ. That doesn't mean the mate becomes a Christian, necessarily. It means the marital partner is under the continual influence of a godly lifestyle, allowing the Holy Spirit to do His wonderful work.

Now, let's return to these scriptural instructions and focus on the words "not under bondage." As you would imagine, that phrase has stirred a storm of controversy. Opinions abound . . . especially regarding bondage . . . to what? Perhaps that's *your* question. You recall the previous chapter's discussion on *severance, permanence, unity,* and *intimacy.* Obviously this section of Scripture has to do with permanence. In marriage the man and woman (so that we're not confused, the Bible clarifies that marriage is to be *only* between a man and a woman) are glued together. The word *bondage* means to be bonded. And, in fact, that is how it's rendered in 1 Corinthians 7:39: "A wife *is bound* as long as her husband lives; but if her husband is dead, she is free to be married to whom she wishes, only in the Lord" (italics added).

By the way, the verse you just read makes it plain that death is another legitimate situation permitting remarriage. That is an obvious truth which warrants no depth of discussion.

I am convinced from a study of this section of Scripture that the Christian partner released by desertion may remarry. Perhaps your unsaved partner has left and closed the door behind him. Quite possibly he has remarried, and therefore you are convinced the bond between the two of you is broken. According to God's Word, being deserted by an unsaved partner frees you to remarry.

Let me add a necessary caution about what it means "to desert" a spouse. We are not talking about having an argument that ends where one stomps out and slams the door. That's not desertion; that's frustration. We've all been there. I've been there and so have you. It's not pleasant, but it is real. Walking away is sometimes the best option. *You do that to avoid murder!* Everyone needs a little space now and then. Desertion, however, means a permanent, willful abandonment of one's spouse. It frequently happens . . . yes, even among Christians.

I will go only that far on this issue of desertion. This is a good place for me to add a note of caution. Be very careful with what you add to the Bible. God is in the long-range, permanent-home and marriage business. It has never been His intention to provide multiple escape routes. Again, please understand that I don't mean to sound harsh or unfair. You may be reading this chapter, still bruised and broken from enduring the tough stuff of a marriage long on the rocks. I can appreciate what you've been enduring. It can get terribly difficult. But unlike ducks, *we* can rationalize any behavior. The burden of proof rests on you. Be certain you can support your plan regarding your unhappy marriage from a careful, conservative interpretation of God's Word. That's the safest route. You can expect God's blessing on your future by following His instructions, not by allowing your emotions to direct your steps and dictate your decisions.

God may want you to stay right where you are to bring about a redemptive outcome in the life of your unbelieving spouse. I've heard many marvelous stories of mates who stayed at it and refused to stop believing and to stop praying. At long last, after years of intense intercession, they joyfully witness the salvation of their mates. But there are just as many cases where no such turnaround occurs. Clearly they have been deserted. In such cases, if your unbelieving mate chooses to walk away for good, you are free to marry another.

Commentator R. C. H. Lenski clearly and concisely addresses this situation:

> From that day onward the fetters of the marriage tie have been broken and remain so, now and indefinitely. The deserting spouse broke them. No law binds the unbelieving spouse. . . .
>
> It goes without saying that a believing spouse will by Christian kindness and persuasion do all that can be done to prevent rupture. But when these fail, Paul's verdict is: "Thou art free!"
>
> Desertion is exactly like adultery in its effect. Both disrupt the marriage tie. . . . The essence of marriage is union. When this is disrupted, the union which God intended to be a permanent one is destroyed, sinfully destroyed. There is only this difference in the case of adultery, the innocent spouse may forgive and continue the marriage, or may accept the dire result, the sundering of the marriage. In the case of desertion the former is not possible; the deserted spouse can no longer continue a marriage, for none exists.[2]

A number of years ago I met a fine Christian lady whose husband, a physician, had deserted her. He was a qualified doctor but a lousy marriage partner. He literally deserted her. She had three small children. She had faithfully stayed by him through hard times only to have him leave without explanation.

Years passed. She eventually met a man whom she had known in high school. He had never married. They fell in love. I had the privilege of marrying them, based on my understanding of the 1 Corinthians 7 teaching regarding desertion. I saw them not long ago, after a few years of marriage, and they could not be happier. The blessing of God was resting on their relationship. Their future is bright. And their marriage is as warm, perhaps stronger, than it has ever been. Together they took God at His Word and without shame followed through with what He permitted.

Remarriage is permitted in the case of marital failure prior to conversion. This next case concerning remarriage is based on two verses in 2 Corinthians 5.

> Therefore from now on we recognize no one according to the flesh; even though we have known Christ according to the flesh, yet now we know Him in this way no longer. Therefore if anyone is in Christ, he is a new creature; the old things passed away; behold, new things have come. (vv. 16–17)

Remember when you were lost? These verses are good reminders of the difference between then and now. You got a fresh start at salvation. Psalm 103:12 states, "As far as the east is from the west, so far has He removed our transgressions from us." Let's apply that to a marriage prior to conversion. In a person's unsaved state, he or she may make a selection for a mate, marry for all the wrong reasons, and the marriage goes belly-up. Some go on to marry again, and again . . . ending up in three or more failed marriages, each ending in divorce. In turn they experience all the horror that accompanies such destructive patterns. Finally, in the bottomless pit of their despair they turn to Christ. They become "new creations." The Greek term translated "new" in this passage is *kainos.* Not new in time, as in recent, but *new in form.* New as in a different nature from what is contrasted as old. When you go to a showroom floor and you buy a *kainos* car, you buy one that's never been driven. It's brand-new. And when an individual is brought from death to life, through faith in Jesus Christ, there is a *kainos* creation. I like the words "a new start." Everything is new. Isn't that magnificent? All the transgressions of yesteryear are forgiven and erased. Yes, A-L-L.

Let me ask you, is divorce a transgression? I never met anybody who says it's not. You may think it's not possible to forgive a divorce. If so, then if it's not forgiven, it's the only transgression that isn't forgiven, which, quite frankly, is illogical. Jesus spoke of a *new* commandment. Paul writes of a *new* self (Ephesians 4:24). The apostle Peter encourages believers to look for *new* heavens and a *new* earth (2 Peter 3:13), in which all righteousness will dwell. All of these are the same *kainos* as used here . . . a *new* creature. In light of that it's my understanding that when you become a Christian you begin your life fresh and anew. Frankly, that's some of the best news I've heard in a long time, don't you agree? Now trust me on this: God can make all things *new*—even a brand-new start in marriage, offering a bright future that once looked bleak because of a broken past. Where sin abounded, grace superabounds!

Some Heads-up Warnings for All Who Are Married—or Who Hope to Be

Remember Mr. and Mrs. Mallard Duck? They were going about their merry way in our backyard, oblivious to the dangers that lurked in the bushes. I repeat, married couples can easily slip into that same sort of naive bliss, ignorant of the inevitable challenges ahead. Because this is true, I want to close the chapter by offering four exhortations to remember in order to protect you and your marriage from slow erosion that could result in a painful demise.

First, to the unmarried: be patient! Some will remain wonderfully content as a single adult all their lives, while others pray, ache, and long for a marriage partner. My exhortation is strong: Don't allow that desire to hurry you into making a commitment you could live to regret. Take the time prayerfully and wisely to choose a mate. I wish I could invite all the impatient singles to come sit in on a heated marriage counseling session. You would quickly change your tune! There are a lot of people who are married to partners they would love for *you* to have. Matter of fact, their partners would say they are readily available! And believe me, you don't want them either. There's something a lot worse than not having a marriage partner, and that's having the wrong one. So, please, be patient.

Second, to the married: be content! God is sovereign. He is at work. And He will be faithful to you regardless of how bleak your situation.

Have you heard about Marriage Anonymous? It's a great joke that is played on soon-to-be brides and grooms. To the groom, Marriage Anonymous sends an old hag in a torn housecoat and curlers. She's really overweight. Furthermore she nags him all through the day, to see if he really wants to get married. To the bride they send a fat, hairy guy in an undershirt, who drinks beer and belches and parks himself in front of a television and sleeps there half the day and into the night. It is amazingly effective!

The point is, keep reality uppermost in your mind. These days "reality TV" distorts the truth. In fact, there's seldom anything *real* about reality TV. Don't rely on Hollywood or television shows to present an accurate view of married life—ever! We get exactly what we put into it. Marriage is not the way it's pictured on the screen. Contentment will come as God gives you the ability to change you, not your spouse. So, please, be content.

Third, to the miserable—I'm referring to you who have the right to end a marriage and remarry: be careful! You are the most vulnerable duck in the pond. You are right on the edge of disaster; because you are so starved for a loving relationship, you're vulnerable to danger. So make all major decisions very slowly. Get wise counsel. Proceed with care. Guard against a free fall. Listen well to a few trustworthy Christian friends. Please be careful.

Fourth, to the remarried: be grateful . . . and understanding! I wish I could say you will find acceptance everywhere you go. I also wish I could guarantee that every church fellowship will throw its arms around you and be happy for you, smiling in affirmation. Don't hold your breath. That may happen . . . it may not. Nevertheless you remain grateful to the Lord for His provision and His matchless grace. Try your best to show understanding toward those who can't see His hand in your happiness. In other words (here we go again!), walk through the tough stuff of remarriage with Christ's hand firmly in yours. He'll teach you and use you and perhaps grow from within you a different kind of ministry that you never dreamed possible.

To you who are remarried—you who had the right to "get a fresh start," enjoy your new relationship. This is the marriage you want to last a lifetime. Cultivate it. Deepen your love. Enjoy your new life! Before God, as you have hammered it out and worked it through, you have every right to the pleasures that are now yours to enjoy.

And may I drop in a few final words to all Christians? *Be extremely discerning.* Be careful with the counsel you give. Don't be too quick to agree that this guy is Mr. Right for your friend because she's so lonely. Instead, lovingly help him or her hold the reins and wait for God's clear leading . . . even if that means living a lifetime without a mate. On the other hand, if a couple has sought spiritual counsel and decide that it is God's will for them to marry—relax and let it be.

Nobody died and left you in charge of their world. Give them your best wishes and loud applause. Who knows? Someday *you* may be there, needing others' understanding and affirmation.

❧

Lord, thank You for Your great grace in our lives . . . in our marriages . . . in our homes. Without Your grace these things would become such a grind. Thank You for love from friends that pulls us through tough stuff— when it's always something. Thank You for wise words from counselors who have assisted us in so many ways. Thank You for Christ, who, single Himself, understood the unmarried life better than anyone else ever could. Thank You for Paul, the great apostle, who no doubt lost his wife or perhaps felt the sting of desertion, who understood that pain. Thank You for the truth of the Bible. We want it to speak louder than any other voice in our mixed-up culture.

Give encouragement and strength to the one who holds this book today and needs clear direction, a fresh touch of grace, and a ton of tender mercy from You. I'd also ask You to bring firm conviction where that's necessary. Finally, dear Father, may we honor You, not because we have to but because we want to.

In the name of Jesus, the one Lord and only Savior, I pray. Amen.

Eight

Getting Through the Tough Stuff of Confrontation

"Experience is the best teacher."[1] You've probably put that familiar maxim to the test and found it quite reliable. Experience certainly removes the foolishness and naiveté of theory. But is that maxim absolutely true? I don't think so. We certainly learn by doing—no question about that. But I think you'd agree, another word is needed to make that an accurate maxim: "*Guided* experience is the best teacher."

If you play a musical instrument, you likely began at an early age, guided by an experienced teacher. When I was a teenager, my oboe instructor was Mr. Valanni, who was a member of the Houston Symphony Orchestra. At the beginning of each weekly lesson, which took place in our home, this fine musician would slowly put his oboe together, I would have mine ready, and then we would begin to play. Only a few notes into the piece and he'd exclaim, "No, no, no, no, no, no!" Which in Italian means, "No, no, no, no, no, no!"

He'd correct my fingering, correct my aperture, or inform me of a better way to "tongue" my notes. Then we'd continue a few more bars, and he would stop us again. Week by week, throughout the year, for forty-five minutes at a crack, Mr. Valanni *guided* me into a more acceptable oboe technique.

The brilliant surgeon has her fellows under her expert guidance; the unflappable pilot guides a young copilot in the precise sequence of preparation for takeoff and/or landing. A renowned soloist schools her pupil in the fine art of a flawless vocal performance.

Guided experience is the best teacher because it adds a crucial and often uncomfortable element to the process: *confrontation*. Confrontation guides the oboe instructor who shows his young student how to form his lips properly across the double reed, the seasoned surgeon who drills her young fellows on the protocol of making a clean incision, or the respected professional who demands repeated attempts at a difficult section of the musical score until the young singer approaches near-perfection.

Sadly, confrontation is usually avoided because it carries such a negative appeal. No one *enjoys* confrontation. I think I've figured out why that is true. It's because we were offended by people in our lives who knew how to *affront* better than *confront*. There's a world of difference. Confrontation is never fun. Getting through the tough stuff of confrontation correctly requires that we gain a solid under-standing of God's perspective on the process. Once again, let's turn to the Scriptures in our pursuit of that perspective.

GAINING AN UNDERSTANDING OF BIBLICAL CONFRONTATION

Interestingly, the word *confrontation* does not appear in the Bible, yet the concept runs like a thread through the biblical story. In fact, I find at least five synonyms throughout the Old and New Testaments that shed light on the idea. To help us begin on the same page, let's look first at four of them found in the book of Proverbs.

Reprove

> He is on the path of life who heeds instruction,
> But he who ignores reproof goes astray. (Proverbs 10:17)

> Whoever loves discipline loves knowledge,
> But he who hates reproof is stupid. (Proverbs 12:1)

No one enjoys a strong reproof. But from time to time we really need it, especially when it comes from God or from someone who is not only qualified but also loves us and has our best interest in view. Great good can come from it. In fact, Proverbs 13:18 teaches, "Poverty and shame will come to him who neglects discipline, but he who regards reproof will be honored."

The second synonym is "rebuke," which is a bit sterner than "reproof," but carries the idea of guided confrontation.

Rebuke

> A rebuke goes deeper into one who has understanding
> Than a hundred blows into a fool. (Proverbs 17:10)

Pound on the body of a fool day after day, month after month, and you'll have little or no impact. But for one who has an understanding, teachable spirit, a tactfully stated rebuke is sufficient.

The third synonym is "wound."

Wound

> Faithful are the wounds of a friend,
> But deceitful are the kisses of an enemy. (Proverbs 27:6)

Confrontation can be a *wounding* experience—it hurts deep down inside. It stings. But when the confronter is a friend, who truly knows and loves us, the benefits are real and lasting.

By the way, not everyone deserves the right to wound us . . . only a close, trustworthy friend—someone like a mentor. Yet some people (especially fellow Christians!) see themselves as having "the gift of confrontation." Legalists are especially given to that kind of thinking. And they are regularly an affront to others. They use a Bible verse to support their caustic, damaging behavior. You and I are much more open to being confronted by someone we trust, someone who loves and cares about us. That's why the very best confrontation comes early between a parent and a child. How essential is guided confrontation in the growing-up years. How unwise are those parents who fail to confront. The loving, grace-filled instruction brought on by the *wounds* of a faithful parent are trustworthy and long-lasting.

A fourth synonym is "correct."

Correct

> Correct your son, and he will give you comfort;
> He will also delight your soul. (Proverbs 29:17)

"Correct" also includes the thought of a confrontation designed to improve one's character. It's the idea of rescuing someone from the wrong path and placing him or her on the correct one.

Finally, the word "discipline" is often a synonym for "confrontation." For a closer look at that word, we need to turn from Proverbs to the book of Hebrews in the New Testament.

Discipline

> It is for discipline that you endure; God deals with you as with sons; for what son is there whom his father does not discipline? But if you are without discipline, of which all have become partakers, then you are illegitimate children and not sons. (Hebrews 12:7–8)

> All discipline for the moment seems not to be joyful, but sorrowful; yet to those who have been trained by it, afterwards it yields the peaceful fruit of righteousness. (v. 11)

Reprove. Rebuke. Wound. Correct. Discipline. Those are terms full of meaning. Contrary to popular opinion, confrontation is an art to be learned and refined. To affront is a quick and dirty tactic. An assault. It comes easily, especially when anger flares. Caustic, critical, cutting people are in abundance. You may be one of those individuals who'd have to confess, "I don't need any lessons on telling people off. I do that in my sleep. Show me something I need to know." If that's you, you need to deal with this more than anyone because you are not confronting; you're assaulting. Put bluntly, that's abuse.

It's that type of misunderstanding that I hope to clear up in this chapter. So much for negatives.

What Confrontation Means

Taken together, all these biblical words help bring focus to what true confrontation should be. Here's how I would define confrontation in a nutshell: *Confrontation is speaking the truth in a personal, face-to-face encounter with someone we love regarding an issue that needs attention or correction.*

Let me repeat, the goal of confrontation is neither to attack nor to cause offense. That's a controlling, spiritual-king-of-the-mountain approach, which never works. No, confrontation is designed to define the issue of concern with the hope of bringing about a needed change with tactfulness and love.

How Confrontation Works

Going through the tough stuff of confrontation requires some deliberate thinking. As I've thought about the process, I've landed on four guiding principles that distill what I believe the Scriptures affirm.

First, state the issue tactfully and directly. Confrontation is rarely done indirectly and seldom done publicly. There must be clear, thoughtful communication delivered firmly but graciously.

Second, provide examples—without exaggeration or a lot of emotion. Examples are stated to prove the point. Something has been going on that cannot continue for certain reasons that must be stated. Point out those things that demonstrate that change has not occurred and then provide specific examples. Be careful to keep your emotions in check. Allow enough time between the offense and the confrontation for prayerful diffusing of any anger, bitterness, and frustration you may feel.

Third, suggest a plan of action. Don't leave the individual you've just confronted to stew and brew without clear direction on how to improve. That's not constructive, and it can lead to more intense issues and unwanted complications. The best approach is simply to identify the problem and then calmly suggest ways the problem can be corrected.

Finally, show compassion and understanding. Don't miss this part! If you do, you will find yourself accusing rather than confronting. Compassion, care, concern, and love are the essential ingredients of a successful confrontation.

These virtues are more easily understood when we see them in action. So once again let's turn to the Master, who all His life regularly had to endure the tough stuff of confrontation—for Him, too, it was always something! Only in this case, it was Peter who routinely needed Christ's firm confronting, which included a series of interventions that eventually formed in him a rugged and resilient faith.

JESUS AND PETER: BIBLICAL CONFRONTATION IN ACTION

As Jesus stepped into the shadow of the cross, His episodes of confrontation increased and intensified. Three passages portray His encounters with Peter—a man whom He deeply loved and who repeatedly expressed devotion to his Master. In each scene we watch Jesus skillfully and lovingly carve away at Peter's character, "taking him from a rough-edged and raw disciple to a perfectly cut stone for the foundation of the church."[2]

When to Confront—Matthew 16:21–23

In the first scene the shadow of the cross looms over Jesus as well as His disciples: "From that time Jesus began to show His disciples that He must go to Jerusalem, and suffer many things from the elders and chief priests and scribes, and be killed, and be raised up on the third day" (v. 21).

The disciples were waiting for Jesus to establish His earthly kingdom—a literal kingdom that would deliver them from the power and oppression of Gentile rule. Christ, the Anointed One, would conquer. Therefore the idea of a suffering Messiah never crossed their minds. Rather than embracing such a concept, they wanted to protect Him from it. Peter, frequently quick to speak his mind, "flung a protective arm around Jesus, as if to hold him back from a suicidal course."[3] Matthew writes, "Peter took Him aside and began to rebuke Him, saying, 'God forbid it, Lord! This shall never happen to You'" (v. 22).

I'm so glad God is no longer recording Scripture, because if He were, most of us would be on its pages, doing many of the same things Peter did. The zealous disciple thought he had Jesus's best interest at heart, but he had the wrong perspective and wound up with his foot in his mouth. His thinking was 180 degrees off course. Jesus wasted no time *or* words confronting Peter and his flawed understanding. "But He turned and said to Peter, 'Get behind Me, Satan! You are a stumbling block to Me; for you are not setting your mind on God's interests, but man's'" (v. 23).

Talk about a strong rebuke! It must have stung, since Peter says nothing in return. I like to think the only thing you might have heard was the stunned disciple's chin hitting his burly chest. Imagine being convinced of your own ardor for Christ and suddenly realizing you're a mouthpiece for the adversary. Like Peter, often we don't know we're mistaken until someone cares enough to confront us. Moments earlier Jesus referred to Peter as the rock on which He would build His church (v. 18). Minutes later the rock reveals an obvious crack as he becomes Satan's spokesman.

"God forbid it, Lord!" "Get behind Me, Satan!" Strong words standing in bold juxtaposition . . . from two who could not have been more intimate as friends. No one ever loved Peter more than the Savior. No one ever saw more potential in Peter than Jesus. That's why He cared enough to confront him.

From this poignant scene I see two answers to the question of *when to confront*. First, we should confront when people become stumbling blocks to us or others and certainly to the gospel. Second, we should confront when people have their minds set on their own interests, rather than God's. Both are worth confrontation.

Let me offer you a little advice at no extra charge. Among your circle of friends, be certain you have a few who care less for your comfort than they do for your character. Most of us want to surround ourselves with friends who make us feel good. Such friends are easy to find. More difficult to find and keep are those friends willing to overlook our comfort for the good of our character, confronting us when we're wrong. A few choice friends like that are invaluable.

Why to Confront —Luke 22:31–34

The second scene is of even greater magnitude than the first, because we're closer to the cross. Jesus's death is imminent and the enemy's working has intensified. In the privacy of the Upper Room, Jesus had just finished a dramatic lesson on what it means to be a servant as He washed the disciples' feet. What He said next, though, must have sent more shock waves through the room as He again directed His words to Peter: "Simon, Simon, behold, Satan has demanded permission to sift you like wheat; but I have prayed for you, that your faith may not fail; and you, when once you have turned again, strengthen your brothers" (vv. 31–32).

Don't rush past that too quickly. Can you imagine being singled out in front of your peers and being told that Satan has a plan just for you? Literally Jesus said, "Satan has begged earnestly for you." In other words, "He wants to have you for himself. He *wants* you!" What's he saying? "Peter, you are in the devil's cross hairs."

You think that still goes on? Do you think Satan's demons are plotting to destroy, or at least spiritually disable, significant people in God's family? Without question. Don't doubt it for a minute! Thankfully the Savior still prays for us (John 17:15; 1 John 2:1). He consistently prays for our preservation and for our strength. There are few words more sobering in all of Scripture than "Satan has begged earnestly to sift you as wheat."

Jesus had all the disciples in mind when He used the plural pronoun "you." When you stop to think about that, He included you and me as well. We would be wise to remember this scene when tempted to go it alone apart from the protection of Christ. Satan would like nothing more than for any one of us to develop an overinflated self-confidence. He rejoices when he sees us independently strutting our stuff. That's when we're most vulnerable, and that's the very trap into which Peter had fallen. We realize his vulnerability when we read Peter's response to Jesus's words: "Lord, with You I am ready to go both to prison and to death!" (v. 33).

In other words, "Lord, bring it on! I can handle *anything* . . . a jail sentence or even death itself. I'm your man."

One of the adversary's most effective techniques is to wait until he can detect in us even a hint of overconfidence—to say nothing of out-and-out arrogance. That is when he moves in for his attacks. When I hear somebody speak of another who has fallen into some awful sin spout forth, "I would never do such a thing!" I shudder. At that very moment, that person is most vulnerable. And so was Peter.

Not surprisingly, Jesus confronted Peter's pious braggadocio: "I say to you, Peter, the rooster will not crow today until you have denied three times that you know Me" (v. 34). Only by God's grace and overcoming power can any of us stand protected against Satan's schemes.

This scene helps us understand *why we confront*. Again, I see two reasons.

First, we confront to strengthen areas of vulnerability. Second, we confront to soften overconfidence—to warn of blind spots. Confronting those we love helps protect them from Satan's sinister assaults and from their own self-destructive overconfidence.

How to Confront—Luke 22:47–62

The final scene opens the night before Christ's agonizing death. To be more precise, it's in the early morning hours of that fateful day. The disciples have eaten their final meal with Jesus. Christ has endured a grueling vigil in the Garden of Gethsemane. Soon the mob emerges from the darkness, their torches flickering in the shadows of the olive trees. Judas, the traitor with murder in his heart, leads the posse. The disciples standing with Jesus grow indignant in His defense: "When those who were around Him saw what was going to happen, they said, 'Lord, shall we strike with the sword?' And one of them struck the slave of the high priest and cut off his right ear" (vv. 49–50).

Would you care to guess the identity of the sword-swinging aggressor who slashed the slave in Christ's defense? Luke doesn't give his name, but John does. You guessed right: Peter, the impetuous one, strikes again (John 18:10). Jesus immediately took control of the situation. In doing so, He confronted the overly aggressive disciple. "But Jesus answered and said, 'Stop! No more of this.' And He touched his ear and healed him" (Luke 22:51).

After confronting Peter, Jesus turned His attention to deal with the venomous band of religious leaders standing ready to apprehend Him:

> Then Jesus said to the chief priests and officers of the temple and elders who had come against Him, "Have you come out with swords and clubs as you would against a robber? While I was with you daily in the temple, you did not lay hands on Me; but this hour and the power of darkness are yours." (vv. 52–53)

Ignoring Jesus's thought-provoking question and straightforward confrontational exposure, the hell-bent accusers arrested Him and dragged Him to the home of the high priest. Not too far behind in the shadows lurked a frightened, halting Peter—once overconfident and presumptuous in his allegiance, now fearing for his life. Slinking through dawn's gray darkness, the stalwart, imposing fisherman from Galilee did what he swore he'd never do—he denied his Lord when pressed for his identity (vv. 54–60). Not once. Not twice. But three separate times—exactly as had been predicted by Jesus only a few hours earlier. At that moment Peter heard the cock crow, and at once he caught the gaze of His Master, whom he had thrice denied. Luke writes, "The Lord turned and looked at Peter. And Peter remembered the word of the Lord, how He had told Him, 'Before a rooster crows today, you will deny Me three times.' And he went out and wept bitterly" (vv. 61–62).

Looking back over these remarkable scenes, I find four methods of confrontation Jesus used to correct Peter and His accusers. They are methods available to us as well.

- An abrupt, passionate command: "Stop! No more of this" (v. 51).
- A thought-provoking question: "Have you come out with swords and clubs as you would against a robber?" (v. 52).

- A well-worded analytical statement: "While I was with you daily in the temple, you did not lay hands on Me; but this hour and the power of darkness are yours" (v. 53).

- A mere glance: "The Lord turned and looked at Peter. And Peter remembered the word of the Lord" (v. 61).

THE NEXT TIME YOU NEED TO CONFRONT

Getting through the tough stuff of confrontation often means resisting the temptation to focus on our own needs, rather than the needs of the one we must confront. In fact, as I've pointed out in the preceding pages, caring for the needs of others should be the basis for any confrontation. David Augsburger, in his book that has helped so many, *Caring Enough to Confront,* refers to the process of confrontation as "care-fronting." I like that expression. He also describes four self-centered approaches to the process of confrontation that you and I must avoid at all cost.

First, there is the aggressive, I'll-get-him approach. That approach carries large doses of revenge and spite toward the offender. Second, there is the scared, I'll-get-out approach. Only frustration and unresolved bitterness await us at the end of that dead-end street. Third, there is the doormat, I'll-give-in method. There's nothing healthy about that approach since it demonstrates a lack of resolve and determination. Fourth, there is the compromising, I'll-meet-you-halfway method, which may sound noble but rarely resolves anything.[4]

I strongly urge that we follow the example of Jesus, who lovingly yet firmly met each confrontation with a fitting resolve. Never shirking from the truth, He always sought to meet the needs of those closest to Him. From His example I find three essentials of what we could call people-affirming, God-honoring confrontation.

First, be sure. Be sure there's a good reason to confront another individual. Confrontations should be rare events. You shouldn't relish the experience. If you find that you do, be concerned enough to stop right there and examine your motives.

Second, be specific. Be specific about the purpose of the confrontation. Don't leave this to speculation. Being vague leads to an uncertain outcome, no matter how tactful and gracious your words. Make certain you know the reason for the confrontation. Then make that reason clear to the person you confront. Spell it out precisely and concisely.

Third, be sensitive. Every situation is different. An extended season of soul-searching prayer must precede any face-to-face confrontation. Without that discipline of reflection you are setting yourself up for an enemy assault. Furthermore the person you're confronting will sense uncertainty and uneasiness in your words. Don't run that risk. If you haven't the time to pray and seek godly counsel on the matter, then don't proceed. Don't push yourself into this on your own. I've seen that type of Clint Eastwood, go-ahead-make-my-day approach too many times to count. Every time, what's left behind is a bloody trail of wounded souls.

This is a good time for me to add: make certain the method you choose fits the needs of the other person by keeping your own personal agenda in check. None of this is about you! Pay attention to timing. Choose your words carefully. And, for sure, pray fervently.

Getting through the tough stuff of confrontation is not easy or simple, especially when it means challenging a person you really love. But if we love someone as dearly and deeply as Christ loved Peter, we won't hold back. We'll care enough to confront.

Nine

Getting Through the Tough Stuff of Pain

Have you seen Mel Gibson's movie *The Passion of the Christ?* It's like none other I've seen. It details the horrifying pain and anguish Jesus suffered in the final hours of His earthly life. By now, millions of viewers around the world have been moved beyond words by the graphic depiction of that violent and shockingly torturous ordeal. People of all ages, cultures, and races have looked on in alarm and disbelief as vivid scenes from the sacred story relentlessly rolled on, growing increasingly more bloody and intense. The film has stirred controversy that is unprecedented in recent history. But why? Why such shock at a story that has been told for centuries? Why the outrage over Gibson's violent interpretation of Christ's final days?

I would answer, *because the film depicts and supports God's revealed Word.*

Many prefer to think of Jesus as meek and mild and gentle at heart. They find quiet rest in the loving Shepherd of Israel, who smiles at children, heals the sick, feeds the hungry, and speaks softly of a kingdom not of this world. Few wish to go much further. They resist embracing His inconceivable pain—His excruciating humiliation, that culminated in a horrible death at the hands of unjust men bent on cursing, cruelty, misery, and murder. No one wishes to dwell on such abject evil.

Yet that is precisely how the Scriptures portray Jesus—a "man of sorrows and acquainted with grief" (Isaiah 53:3).

The Bible swells with more appealing and endearing prospects of the Savior. They are the names we love to let fall from our lips in song and in prayerful devotion: Prince of Peace, Lord of Hosts, the Good Shepherd, the Great Physician, Morning Star, Lion of Judah, Lamb of God.

But *Man of Sorrows?* That doesn't sound like anyone we'd care to get close to, does it? Until we find ourselves in the crucible of the tough stuff of pain. Enveloped in a world of hurt, broken by life's brutal blows, we discover He's everything we need.

COMING TO AN UNDERSTANDING OF PAIN

Long before Mel Gibson even thought about making a movie that dramatically focused on the passion of Christ, the prophet Isaiah wrote his original script. It would serve as the basis of a drama to unfold nearly eight centuries later. Isaiah, under the inspiration of the Holy Spirit, wrote of God's promised Messiah—the One above all others who understands your pain and mine—the Man of Sorrows.

As It Relates to Jesus's Life

Normally we don't think of the Messiah in terms of weakness, sadness, deep sorrow, and grief. Yet Isaiah describes Him precisely in that manner, using just about every synonym available for suffering. Read slowly and thoughtfully the ancient prophet's penetrating prophecy.

> He was despised and rejected of men, a man of sorrows and acquainted with grief; and like one from whom men hide their face He was despised, and we did not esteem Him. Surely our griefs He Himself bore, and our sorrows He carried; yet we ourselves esteemed Him stricken, Smitten of God, and afflicted. But He was pierced through for our transgressions, He was crushed for our iniquities; the chastening for our well-being fell upon Him, and by His scourging we are healed. (Isaiah 53:3–5)

> He was oppressed and He was afflicted, yet He did not open His mouth; like a lamb that is led to slaughter, and like a sheep that is silent before its shearers, so He did not open His mouth. (v.7)

> But the LORD was pleased to crush Him, putting Him to grief. . . . As a result of the anguish of His soul, He will see it and be satisfied; by His knowledge the Righteous One, My Servant, will justify the many, as He will bear their iniquities. (vv. 10–11)

That doesn't sound like a milquetoast Messiah to me, wouldn't you agree? No, Jesus endured, and therefore He understands the depth of human pain and suffering. Look again at a list of Isaiah's words: despised, griefs, sorrows, crushed, oppressed, afflicted, scourged, pierced through, smitten, stricken, like a lamb led to slaughter. Today we would say, He's been there . . . done that, even though we don't like to think about it. We like to think of Messiah as winning, not losing. We want to see Him in white garments coming on a white horse. We like Him to be conquering and victorious. But that is not the way He was predicted to be.

The writer of the New Testament book of Hebrews picks up the theme of Christ's suffering when he writes, "In the days of His flesh, He offered up both prayers and supplications with loud crying and tears to the One able to save Him from death, and he was heard because of His piety" (Hebrews 5:7). I find that to be a remarkably comforting thought. The Son of God, in all His deity, being also fully human, felt the sting of impending death and called on His heavenly Father for comfort and help.

Stop and think about what you've just read. All of it has to do with pain—that four-letter word from which we try our best to escape. But Jesus deliberately did not choose that route. He accepted the pain, He endured it, and He embraced it. *Webster's Dictionary* defines physical pain as "a basic bodily sensation induced by a noxious stimulus, received by naked nerve endings, characterized by physical discomfort . . . acute mental or emotional distress."[1] Jesus knew such physical and emotional pain, as we shall discover in the pages that follow. Being the Man of Sorrows that he was, He understands and identifies with our deepest hurts and struggles.

If there is anyone who can meet you in your pain, you have found Him in the prophet Isaiah's *Man of Sorrows.*

As It Relates to Our Lives

You and I enter this world screaming. Physicians tell us that one of the first signs of good, healthy lungs in newborns is that initial, piercing cry. The tiny child whose little frame has only moments before squeezed its way through a narrow birth canal screeches in pain when it leaves the warmth of the womb and emerges with a gush into the cold, cruel world—a world of pain.

From the moments we're born until our final breaths, pain is our companion, albeit one we'd choose to abandon. Still, pain does have its benefits. Physically, for instance, pain signals unseen trouble, and it helps caring mothers and physicians pinpoint the problem. Personally, just like Christ, we learn obedience from the things we suffer (Hebrews 5:8). Spiritually, the pain of adversity helps us grow into mature people of faith (James 1:2–4).

Philip Yancey, in his insightful work *Where Is God When It Hurts?* writes,

> I have never read a poem extolling the virtues of pain, nor seen a statue erected in its honor, nor heard a hymn dedicated to it. Pain is usually defined as "unpleasantness."
>
> Christians don't really know how to interpret pain. If you pinned them against the wall, in a dark, secret moment, many Christians would probably admit that pain was God's one mistake. He really should have worked a little harder and invented a better way of coping with the world's dangers.
>
> I am convinced that pain gets a bad press. Perhaps we should see statues, hymns, and poems to pain. Why do I think that? Because up close, under a microscope, the pain network is seen in an entirely different light. It is perhaps the paragon of creative genius.[2]

Emotional or mental pain is not quite as objective. Almost always on target, C. S. Lewis adds this comment, "Mental pain is less dramatic than physical pain, but it is more common and also more hard to bear. It is easier to say 'My tooth is aching' than to say 'My heart is broken.' . . . Sometimes, however, it persists, and the effect is devastating."[3]

I love that quote! In other words, it's hard enough to go to a dentist when I have a bad tooth, but where do I go with this broken heart? I suggest the answer is not that difficult: We go to Jesus, the Man of Sorrows, who is acquainted with grief, who understands our brokenness and pain. Pain has a way of turning us back to the Savior. That makes it essential for our growth and spiritual well-being. If you're feeling despised, forsaken, rejected, crushed, or afflicted, Jesus understands (Hebrews 4:15). To what degree does He understand?

To answer that, let's revisit those final hours of Jesus's life and look closely at the categories of pain He suffered.

THE PAIN OF GETHSEMANE AND THE ANGUISH OF THE CROSS

At the commencement of Christ's ministry John the Baptist pointed to Him and said, "Behold, the Lamb of God who takes away the sin of the world!" (John 1:29). I've often imagined the dull sense of dread those words must have sent through Christ's soul—knowing He'd one day be the actual "Lamb led to the slaughter." Yet His physical suffering was only a portion of the cup of suffering He would be compelled to drink.

Relational Pain

Matthew 26:30 tells us that Jesus and His disciples had just completed their final meal together, which they ended by singing a hymn. That must have been an extremely emotional time for the Savior, as He reflected on the torturous anguish He'd soon endure and those He'd be forced to leave behind. The men He had lived among for so many months knew nothing of what would soon unfold. But Jesus knew what was ahead of Him from that moment all the way to the cross. If there was ever a time when He needed the strong support of His closest friends, it was in those ominous hours in Gethsemane.

Then Jesus came with them to a place called Gethsemane, and said to His disciples, "Sit here while I go over there and pray." And He took with Him Peter and the two sons of Zebedee, and began to be grieved and distressed. Then He said to them, "My soul is deeply grieved, to the point of death; remain here and keep watch with Me." (Matthew 26:36–38)

Gethsemane. The word means "oilpress." Symbolically it is easy to see how it represents those places of deep, pressing pain and mental agony. We each have our own Gethsemane to endure. Perhaps you are in the depth of yours today. Maybe not; for you it could be in the future. Maybe you've passed through one and before you could catch your breath you've entered another. It's always something! It's at those times that having a few close friends means the most. We lean on them and draw strength from them.

In one of the most intimate scenes from Jesus's life, Matthew writes of the Savior inviting His closest friends to remain with Him as a ready source of encouragement and support: "And He went a little beyond them, and fell on His face and prayed, saying, 'My Father, if it is possible, let this cup pass from Me; yet not as I will, but as You will'" (v. 39). Christ's pain was so intense He pleaded with His Father for a way out of it. Don't hurry over that. In Luke's Gospel, we're told that Jesus prayed with such intensity that He dripped sweat that "became like drops of blood" oozing from his skin and falling to the ground (Luke 22:44).

Drenched in pain's agony, Jesus returned to His friends in hopes of finding some needed encouragement. But in that time, when He needed them the most, His disciples failed Him miserably. Read carefully through this tender but convicting scene, and allow Matthew's words to touch you deeply. Let your heart be broken.

And He came to the disciples and found them sleeping, and said to Peter, "So, you men could not keep watch with Me for one hour? Keep watching and praying that you may not enter into temptation; the spirit is willing, but the flesh is weak."

He went away again a second time and prayed, saying, "My Father, if this cannot pass away unless I drink it, Your will be done." Again He came and found them sleeping for their eyes were heavy. And He left them again, and went away and prayed a third time, saying the same thing once more. Then He came to the disciples and said to them, "Are you still sleeping and resting? Behold, the hour is at hand and the Son of Man is being betrayed into the hands of sinners. Get up, let us be going; behold the one who betrays Me is at hand!"(Matthew 26:40–46)

Each time Jesus returned to His friends, they lay snoozing in the grass. What a pathetic scene. To make things worse, as we saw in the previous chapter, one of His close companions stood ready to betray Him publicly. Jesus knelt in Gethsemane, broken in spirit and betrayed, anguished of soul and grieving, missing the comfort of those He had mentored for over three years. Truly alone, He now experienced the deep, relational pain of failed friendships and would soon feel the kiss of the traitor.

There is no place more alone than one's own Gethsemane. Support groups are great. I believe in them and encourage every one of them in our church. But there are personal Gethsemanes you must walk through completely alone. You'll always feel a deep loneliness while you're getting through the tough stuff of pain. That's when Christ will be there. Your best friends may fail you. Some will try to understand, but often they can't. A few, frankly, will forget you. Some may turn against you. In the agony of your need for relational support, you'll have *all you need* with Christ. You will find Him at those times closer than a brother. I know. He has met me in my own Gethsemanes, and He will do so again and again and yet again.

Internal Pain

A good friend of mine and former fellow church staff team member, David Carder, has spent years counseling brokenhearted people. Dave offers a rare insight into the reality of internal pain as he observes, "Knowing doesn't automatically fix feelings." Isn't that an excellent insight?

In spite of the fact that Jesus knew all His life He would suffer a horrible death on the cross, such knowledge did not remove the internal agony He endured when the zero hour arrived.

Jesus had known for thirty-three years that the cup of suffering would come. Knowing all of that for so long didn't fix His feelings of intense pain. When the full weight landed on Him at Gethsemane, He pleaded for relief.

Herein lies a vital lesson for all of us: we are never more presumptuous than when we try to give hurting people the feelings we think *they ought to have* in their anguish. Don't dare invade that tender, internal space! There are occasions when another's anguish is essential for the accomplishment of God's plan. Even though some of us wish to rescue others from pain, we need to restrain ourselves from doing so. Let's guard against cutting in on God's plan. Don't try to fix people's feelings. Our best involvement is usually to "keep watch and pray." To stay near and be silent. To be available and to support.

Jesus understands better than anyone the silent cries of your internal pain.

Physical Pain

For those who have seen *The Passion of the Christ*, I need not rehearse in detail the depth of physical pain Christ endured. The brutalities were horrific and like none experienced by anyone before or since. A quick glance at Matthew's list provides an overview of the intensity of what Christ experienced physically.

- He was seized and treated harshly like a common criminal (Matthew 26:57).

- He was spit on in the face, slapped, and beaten (26:67).

- He was bound and scourged, according to the other Gospel writers (27:2; Mark 15:15; John 19:1).

- He was spit on again and mercilessly beaten with a reed (Matthew 27:30).

- He was crucified, spikes driven into His hands and feet, and later a sword was thrust into His side (27:33–35; John 19:34).

Imagine the horror of having iron spikes pounded into your hands and into your feet. Or the excruciating humiliation of being hung naked in plain view of a gawking crowd. Insects no doubt swarmed His bloodsoaked body. It must have been a horrible event to witness, to say nothing of personally enduring it!

Christ's body had been so mutilated He didn't even look human. The physical pain He must have borne is nothing short of mind-boggling. Still there was a pain more severe than that which He felt physically. Thankfully because of Christ it's a pain you and I will never know.

The Ultimate Pain—Separation from God

Though Christ's relational, internal, and physical pain were horribly intense, the pain of being separated from His Father goes far beyond our ability to imagine. Matthew writes, "Now from the sixth hour darkness fell upon all the land until the ninth hour. About the ninth hour Jesus cried out with a loud voice, saying, '*Eli, Eli, Lama Sabachthani?*' that is, 'My God, My God, why have You forsaken Me?'" (Matthew 27:45–46).

For the first and only time, God turned His back on His Son. It was at that moment Christ bore all *our* sin. That's why the Father could not look on Him—because of the affront of our iniquities. Christ experienced the ultimate pain—separation from God the Father. In absolute loneliness and pain Jesus screamed, "Why have You forsaken Me?"

Let me assure you, you cannot have a heartache that Jesus doesn't understand and with which He doesn't identify. You cannot have a physical pain that somehow escapes His awareness. You cannot have a crippling disease, a disability, a grief, a heart attack . . . not even a debilitating fear or panic attack that He cannot understand or feel.

He's felt it all. Therefore He's there to walk with you through your most profound depths of pain, if you'll only let Him.

Do you have a lingering scar on your heart that won't heal? Look at His hands, His feet, and His side. Feeling humiliated and alone? He knows what that feels like. Are you so confused by your circumstances that you're tempted to bargain with God for relief? No need. Without one word from your lips, He understands. He's touched with the feelings of our weaknesses, and therefore He identifies with them.

Perhaps you're lonely. Your lifelong mate has gone to be with the Lord. You face an uncertain future—all alone. You may have recently been forgotten. Your parents told you to get out of their lives. Perhaps your husband or your wife just walked out for good, rejecting you for someone else. Or you may have just read a cruel letter from an adult child that included seven words you cannot bear to believe: "I never want to see you again." Relationally, you need somebody. Internally, you're in anguish. Physically, you've reached your threshold.

You may be confused, living with deep emotional scars as a result of being abused. You may suffer from such a horrible and shameful addiction that you fear rejection by anyone who might discover your secret. The pain of shame grips your soul and ambushes your thoughts. Perhaps you feel helpless, enraged, confused, disappointed, depressed, misunderstood, humiliated, and at the end.

Ultimately you wonder, as Jesus did, why God has forsaken *you*. You may feel that, but hear this: you are not alone. There is hope. There is help with the Savior by your side.

Getting Through the Tough Stuff of Pain . . . with Christ

I want to close this chapter with several analogies I hope will provide you a measure of comfort as you walk with Christ through the tough stuff of your pain.

Relationally, no one stays closer than Christ. Christ is better than the most faithful husband, more understanding than the most comforting wife, more reliable than the choicest friend. No one stays closer than Christ. There is no friend more caring. There is no person more unconditionally accepting. There is no one more available or more interested whom you can talk to in the middle of the night, or at any other time, simply by calling out in prayer. He even understands your groanings—He's able to put correct meanings to your inexpressible moans! He has promised never to leave you. He will not walk out on you. No one stays closer than Christ. I'll say it again: *no one.*

Internally, no one heals deeper than Christ. You may say, "I'll never be able to get over this grief." Yes you can, but not on your own. That's where Christ is the Master Comforter. He's the "Man of Sorrows." Remember, He is intimately "acquainted with grief." He understands what there is to lose. He lost everything for you. His own family thought He was insane. Right in the middle of His ministry they came to take Him away because they were convinced He was losing his senses (go back and glance through chapter 2, "Getting Through the Tough Stuff of Misunderstanding"). He knows what it feels like to suffer in silence, to be the brunt of unfair criticism, to feel helpless when no one understands, when no one remains in your corner. His balm of comfort penetrates. No one heals deeper than Christ.

Physically, no one comforts better than Christ. In the midst of your deepest physical pain, His presence brings comfort and strength. He may choose to restore your physical health, but frankly, He may not. Regardless, His grace is abundantly sufficient for you. His hand is on your life at this time of your affliction. It's better than the hand of any friend, any partner, any parent, or any child, because when He touches, He brings great compassion and lasting relief. No one comforts better than Christ.

Ultimately, no one sees the benefits of our pain clearer than Christ. He sees through the dark, winding tunnel of your Gethsemane all the way to the end. You see only the unrelenting, frightening, thick darkness. He sees beyond it into the shining light of eternity. Maturity, growth, stability, wisdom, and ultimately the crown of life await the one who trusts His unseen hand. Keep in mind, He owns the map that gets you through your Gethsemane. No one sees the benefits of our pain clearer than Christ.

Whatever you're facing today, please remind yourself that your pain is no mistake. It is no accident. In fact, your suffering may be precisely what Christ will use to bring you to your knees, to draw you back to His heart and discover His peace.

"Man of Sorrows," what a name! It's the name of the Son of God. His name is Jesus. It's the name that represents the extremes of pain and understanding, companionship and relief. Perhaps you have never recognized your need for a personal relationship with God, through faith in Christ. You've gripped the reins of your life tightly in your own hands. I suggest you release them and turn them over to God. Come to His Son, Jesus. Admit where you are and express to him what you need. A simple prayer is all it takes to begin this life-transforming relationship with Him. I close with a simple prayer you may use to speak in the quietness of your heart to the One who longs to walk with you through the tough stuff of personal pain.

> *Lord Jesus,*
>
> *I know that I'm a sinner. I've made a royal mess of my life.*
> *I'm tired of the fight. I'm tired of the flight. I'm tired of the pain I've*
> *added to my life by living as if You didn't exist. Today, I come to You,*
> *believing that You died for me and that You rose from the dead. I turn*
> *my back on my stubborn ways as I surrender all to You. Take the reins,*
> *Lord Jesus. I release them to You. I accept Your forgiveness, and I claim*
> *Your grace, as I accept your gift of eternal life. Amen.*

HALLELUJAH, WHAT A SAVIOR!
Philip R. Bliss

"Man of Sorrows!" what a name
For the Son of God, who came
Ruined sinners to reclaim!
Hallelujah, what a Savior!

Bearing shame and scoffing rude,
In my place condemned He stood—
Sealed my pardon with His blood:
Hallelujah, what a Savior!

Guilty, vile and helpless we,
Spotless Lamb of God was he;
Full atonement! Can it be?
Hallelujah, what a Savior![4]

Ten

Getting Through the Tough Stuff of Prejudice

Early in the tumultuous 1960s, many people were shocked by the controversial book *Black Like Me*. The book's author, John Howard Griffin, was a white man who told the true story of how he became a black man to prove a point.

Through a series of experiments and unusual treatments, Griffin temporarily changed his skin color from white to black. He then moved throughout several of the states in the Deep South and experienced the ugliest side of prejudice. The book chronicles what Griffin experienced. He found that people, who earlier had treated him with respect and common courtesies when his skin was white, subjected him to humiliating mistreatment, insults, and a vile disregard that could only be described as hatred simply because his skin was black.

What that author experienced on his lonely endeavor was a frightening journey into the tough stuff of prejudice. One need only read a few words of the preface to his book to sense the impact of what he felt.

> The Negro. The South. These are the details. The real story is the universal one of men who destroy the souls and bodies of other men (and in the process destroy themselves) for reasons neither really understands. It is the story of the persecuted, the defrauded, the feared and detested. I could have been a Jew in Germany, a Mexican in a number of states, or a member of any "inferior" group. Only the details would have differed. The story would be the same.[1]

By the way, prejudice can be found on both sides. There are Jews against Palestinians and Palestinians against Jews. Muslims against Christians and Christians against Muslims. Conservatives against liberals and liberals against conservatives. Males against females and females against males. On and on prejudice goes, transcending every culture, continent, and race.

Read carefully the closing words of the preface to *Black Like Me*—the words of a man who went deep into the underbelly of America's prejudiced past and emerged a prophet for future generations.

> This may not be all of it. It may not cover all the questions, but it is what it is like to be a Negro in a land where we keep the Negro down.
>
> Some whites will say this is not really it. They will say this is the white man's experience as a Negro in the South, not the Negro's.
>
> But this is picayunish, and we no longer have time for that. We no longer have time to atomize principles and beg the ques-

tion. We fill too many gutters while we argue unimportant points and confuse issues. . . .

This began as a scientific research study of the Negro in the South, with careful compilation of data for analysis. But I filed the data, and here publish the journal of my own experience living as a Negro. I offer it in all its crudity and rawness. It traces the changes that occur to heart and body and intelligence when a so-called first-class citizen is cast on the junkheap of second-class citizenship.[2]

Don't rush past that last phrase, which I believe captures the essence of prejudice: *when a so-called first-class citizen is cast on the junkheap of second-class citizenship.* That's what prejudice of any form or degree does—it degrades humans, categorizing them in essence as *junk.*

We all harbor secret, perhaps even blatant, prejudices. Often those attitudes run so deep within our hearts we become extremely uncomfortable even reflecting on the notion of it.

Philosopher William James wrote that as humans, our natural tendency is to "keep unaltered as much of our old knowledge, as many of our old prejudices and beliefs, as we can. We patch and tinker more than we renew."[3]

But patching and tinkering will not suffice, not for our purposes here. Perhaps you've experienced firsthand the anguish and shame of prejudice. Maybe you're enduring the damaging and hostile attitudes or actions of prejudice these days. Truth be told, you may be facing the ugly presence of prejudice in your own life for the first time, and you are determined not only to come to terms with it but to conquer it. Good for you! Jesus Christ is One who endured it and lives now to walk with you through that process. With His help, I'm convinced you can move to a point in your life where you will be renewed and transformed. I'm referring to every shred of prejudice in your heart being *removed*, not merely patched over and tinkered with.

PREJUDICE DEFINED AND OBSERVED

Jesus made it painfully clear that prejudice is a heart problem. He said,

> For from within, out of the heart of men, proceed the evil thoughts, fornications, thefts, murders, adulteries, deeds of coveting and wickedness, as well as deceit, sensuality, envy, slander, pride and foolishness. All these evil things proceed from within and defile the man. (Mark 7:21–23)

That just about covers the waterfront of sinful attitudes, don't you agree? You don't see the word "prejudice" included in Christ's list, yet the evil attitude it represents would be a part of such phrases as "evil thoughts," and "pride and foolishness." Prejudice comes from deep within the sinful, depraved heart of humanity. It begins there and then works its way into evil actions that can lead to violent aggression.

General Definitions

My definition of *prejudice* would be "any preconceived judgment or irrational attitude of hostility directed against an individual, a group, a race." It would include what others may believe. So to be prejudiced is to judge prematurely, to form an opinion strictly on the basis of preconceived ideas. Prejudice has a blinding effect on its victims.

General Observations

I've observed prejudice for years, having been raised in the South. As a matter of fact, I lived all of my formative years in the South. But prejudice is not reserved to any particular region of the country or limited to a certain culture. It is a prevalent evil that plagues all people everywhere on every continent across the planet.

As I have confronted it and even experienced its sting, I've observed three general principles about prejudice.

First, prejudice is a learned trait. I wasn't born prejudiced. Neither were you. Like you, I was born in sin, and therefore I learned prejudiced attitudes and feelings. We are taught it by our peers, our parents, and most often those older than we.

I know prejudice. It's a shameful thing. It's a heartbreaking thing. The mental assault and emotional harm it causes go beyond imagination. The years I was involved with the U.S. Marine Corps, including training alongside fellow recruits, helped a great deal as I prepared for combat. I quickly realized it didn't matter in the heat of battle whether the one fighting next to me was black, Asian, white or Hispanic . . . male or female. As long as he or she could hold a rifle and fire it accurately in the opposite direction of me, I didn't care about skin color or cultural roots or political preferences.

Still, deep down I have to fight prejudice as do you. I can't just patch and tinker. I have to have a mind that has been completely renewed.

Second, prejudice blinds us in great darkness. In Matthew 6:22–23, Jesus explained that "the eye is the lamp of the body; so then if your eye is clear, your whole body will be full of light. But if your eye is bad, your whole body will be full of darkness."

Our eyes are like windows. They allow light to enter, and the light forms an image resulting in the miracle of sight. Our brains then transform that image into thoughts and concepts and ideas. That's not only true physically; it's also true emotionally and spiritually.

If the eye sees a skin color that is different or some cultural expression that it doesn't understand or value, an opinion or prejudgment is formed that impacts the whole person—body, mind, and will. The mind blindly bases its judgments on a reality that is, at best, dimly perceived.

Third, prejudice binds us to the old. Prejudice is the ugliest side of traditionalism. You rarely find a prejudiced person who is also innovative and creative. It's remarkable how creativity and innovation go along with a more progressive and broad-minded philosophy of life. Prejudice closes our minds to the possibility of the unusual. It holds our thoughts hostage in the vise grip of habit.

PREJUDICE IN JESUS'S DAY

Prejudice frequently reared its ugly head in Jesus's day. He often felt its sting and shame. That's why you want Him by your side as you endure the tough stuff of prejudice, because He's experienced all its forms and fury.

Geographical Prejudice

In the first century the Holy Land was only one hundred and twenty miles long. Galilee sat in the northernmost territory. Located in the southern region was Judea. Across the central section stretched the territory of Samaria. The Jewish people hated the Samaritans so severely that they refused to travel through the Samaritan country, choosing instead to go completely around it, even though the detour doubled their travel time. Nevertheless those who considered it a gross insult to be contaminated by Samaritan dust, believed the extra time was well worth the effort. Going *around* Samaria became a way of life for the Jews.

Jesus remained above the racial fray but encountered the tension on one occasion while He rested at a well in the village of Sychar in Samaria. When He asked a Samaritan woman for a drink, she was absolutely shocked. She responded, incredulously, "How is it that You, being a Jew, ask me for a drink since I am a Samaritan woman?" (John 4:9). She knew the drill. No Jew even *looked* at a Samaritan, to say nothing of *speaking* to one!

In another astonishing scene John describes a confrontation Jesus had with the Pharisees. They were snarling at Him for claiming to be the Son of God. Jesus exclaimed in John 8, "I speak the things which I have seen with My Father; therefore you also do the things which you heard from your father. . . . But because I speak the truth, you do not believe Me" (vv. 38, 45). At that, the whole lot of them threw their heads back and howled, "Do we not say rightly that You are a Samaritan and have a demon?" (v. 48). Imagine the insult of that prejudiced remark spoken to the Son of God! It was as if they cursed Him. Prejudice dripped from their accusation. Jesus neither had a demon, nor was He a Samaritan; yet the Pharisees accused Him of both. Remember, as you read through the New Testament, there were those feuding territories, those unwritten prejudices, not unlike the Hatfields and McCoys of yesteryear. Jesus faced them continually.

The Samaritan woman's words and the vicious verbal assaults of the Pharisees betray the fact that the first-century Jews had fallen into the grip of intense geographical and cultural prejudice. A more intense *political* prejudice existed, though, between the Jewish people and the Romans.

Political Prejudice

Palestine in the first century lay under Roman rule. It was an occupied land, not a respected state or independent nation. Jews in Palestine lived under the Roman boot, operating their everyday existence under the authority of Caesar. Not surprisingly, the Jewish people loathed the oppression. To them there was only One to whom they would pledge their allegiance as King, and it certainly wasn't Caesar. They considered their nation a theocracy, ruled by Yahweh, the Maker of heaven and earth. God's law was sacred to them, not the laws of Rome. But they were forced to pay homage to the godless monarchy of an unbelieving, Gentile authority in Rome. As you can imagine, the political prejudice between the two was off the charts. Each despised the other.

Playing off this known prejudice, the Pharisees attempted to embroil Jesus in one of the hot political conflicts of that day when they asked Him, "Tell us then, what do You think? Is it lawful to give a poll-tax to Caesar, or not?" (Matthew 22:17).

There were three taxes in those days. First was a ground tax, which was one-tenth of everyone's grain and one-fifth of everyone's oil and wine, paid back in kind or in cash. Second, there was income tax. One percent of everyone's income was paid to Rome. Third, there was the poll tax. Every male person from ages fourteen to sixty-five and every female person from ages twelve to sixty-five paid a denarius (a little more than a day's wages) to Caesar. The tribute coin bore the mark of Caesar. Let the scene unfold slowly in your mind as Matthew describes it.

> Then the Pharisees went and plotted together how they might trap Him in what He said. And they sent their disciples to Him, along with the Herodians, saying, "Teacher, we know that

You are truthful and teach the way of God in truth, and defer to no one; for You are not partial to any. Tell us then, what do You think? Is it lawful to give a poll-tax to Caesar, or not?"

But Jesus perceived their malice, and said, "Why are you testing Me, you hypocrites? Show Me the coin used for the poll-tax." And they brought Him a denarius. And He said to them, "Whose likeness and inscription is this?" They said to Him, "Caesar's." Then He said to them, "Then render to Caesar the things that are Caesar's; and to God the things that are God's." (vv. 15–21)

What a brilliant answer! As Jesus held that coin in His hand, He looked at the head then looked at the tail. The head read, "Tiberius Caesar, son of the divine Augustus" on one side. The tail read, "Pontiff Maximus, the High Priest." That alone made the Pharisees' blood boil. In their minds only Caiaphus bore the title "high priest," not some filthy Roman politician! That scene goes a long way in helping us understand the intensity of the political prejudice prevalent in Jesus's day.

Still another level of prejudice was present—religious prejudice in its most violent form.

Religious Prejudice and the Trials and Death of Jesus

Do you realize the people initially responsible for putting Christ on the cross were the Jewish leaders? It was the Pharisees, scribes, and Sadducees. That's not an anti-Semitic statement; that's a historical fact. Together they plotted to rid the land of Jesus, the alleged Messiah, and His pathetic, fanatical delusions.

Now, understand, the Jewish law prohibited death by crucifixion.

Crucifixion was a Roman means of execution, reserved for the vilest offenders, thieves, murderers, and insurgents. That alone ate away at the Jews. The fact that they were compelled to bring their accused and convicted before a Roman official belittled their deepest religious conviction. They hated the Romans for that and numerous other limitations placed on their sacred law.

So ultimately it was the Romans who literally nailed Jesus to the cross, not the Jewish people.

That explains why the Jewish leaders had to bring Jesus to Pilate, the governor of Judea. It also explains why they had to trump up the charge against Jesus. In Jewish law, to be guilty of blasphemy is punishable by death, but Roman law carried no such condemnation. So when Christ's prejudiced accusers brought Him before the Roman authorities, they changed the accusation to treason. They contended that He was claiming to be king of the Jews. That charge was never brought before any Jewish court during the kangaroo trials that led up to Christ's death. But it becomes especially significant when He appears before Pilate. Anyone in Rome who attempted to set himself up to be king would be arrested and condemned to death.

That's why Jesus finally appeared before Pilate. He loathed the Jewish people and the arrogance with which they maintained their self-righteous, petty, and tedious religious ways. Jews were inferior to the Roman mind. Interestingly Pilate is a puppet, operating under the threat of the Jews around him and the possibility of being removed from office because of many complaints against him. He is a prejudiced man who, for unexplainable reasons, looked at Jesus with some ambivalence and perhaps a bit of respect. He did his duty and questioned Jesus about their charge and many others, but in the end he found nothing to suggest the charges of his accusers had any merit.

Pilate's efforts to free Jesus, however, failed because of the fierce insistence of the riotous mob, who willingly accepted the responsibility of Jesus's death (Matthew 27:25–26).

Jesus said hardly a word throughout the agonizing ordeal. He remained silent, refusing to answer a single charge leveled against Him (26:63; 27:12, 14).

But, strangely, Pilate is the only man who comes anywhere near giving Jesus an appropriate trial. He examines Him and finds nothing wrong. Pilate saw through the whole mess. He realized he had on his hands a man with trumped up charges against Him. Tragically he's too weak stand alone and obey his conscience. He asks, "What evil has He done?" You can almost hear the desperation in his words. Finally Pilate pleaded, "What shall I do with Jesus who is called Christ?" (27:22). The mob screamed back in response, "Crucify Him!" (v. 23).

You wonder the extent of prejudice? You just read it in two words. Actually it's only one word in the Greek text, "*Crucify!*"

A life honed on murderous hatred is driven by a heart full of prejudice. Prejudice reduces the human spirit to the level of a killer beast.

I shudder when I think of what that scene was like when it happened. What about the children of those enraged people whose prejudice and hatred for Christ erupted in such violence? Many of the children were not old enough to know what was happening, but be certain the prejudice passed on. The hatred absorbed into their brains. To this day most of the Jewish people reject Jesus as their promised Messiah. In fact, usually the more orthodox they are, the more intense is their rejection.

How did Jesus endure the tough stuff of prejudice? He kept silent. He made no answer. He refused to defend Himself. He endured their abuse, their insults, and their obscenities. Even when their foul-smelling saliva ran down His bruised and bloody body, He remained quiet.

WHAT ABOUT YOU? WHAT ABOUT ME?

Now if you think John Howard Griffin's story in *Black Like Me* is shocking, what Christ experienced at the hands of bigoted, hate-filled, prejudiced men boggles the mind. The perfect Son of God laid aside the independent and voluntary use of His divine attributes as He came to this earth to die, agreeing to pay the price for the sins of prejudiced people—not only theirs, but yours and mine as well. "Amazing love—how can it be?" All from a man who Himself never entertained one prejudicial thought.

I have no idea where your prejudices lie. I know nothing of your background. But I know the human heart, and I know my own especially, as you know yours. I know that it's impossible to escape the subtle, if not altogether overt, teachings of prejudiced people who are older than we or who may be determined to shape our thinking, prompting us to form hurtful opinions of others.

I must remind you that Christ died for the sin of prejudice. He experienced the sting of its assault. He endured the cursing remarks; He felt the shame of rejection; He faced the shocking alienation of hatred. That had to hurt, even for Him.

That's why I'm able to write with such confidence that Jesus is there for you in your suffering of prejudice. He's there to offer His comforting presence and tender words of assurance when your faith falters under unfair discrimination and gross injustice. When you meet Him in the tough stuff of prejudice, He points out those blind spots in your own spiritual sight that keep you from seeing the truth. If you allow Him the freedom to do so, He will soften your spirit toward people of another color, another culture, another sexual preference or religion.

How easy for us as Americans to allow the anger and rage we feel against the perpetrators of the horrors of September 11, 2001, to churn into a brooding hatred and prejudice against all Muslims. Jesus offers a better way in which to treat our Muslim neighbors: "Love your neighbor as yourself." Five simple words packed with compassion and understanding.

He gives you another way in which to view people who believe very differently than you. When His love infuses your veins, it's like fresh blood that makes you virtually color-blind and more tolerant and accepting of people who are different from you. That does not mean you must embrace something you don't believe or take on behaviors you cannot condone. Jesus strikes a perfect balance. He's able to lead you across the barriers and walls you've constructed over the years and use you to reach a lost and lonely soul or a wayward and wandering child of God. He's in the process of doing that with me.

Some Concluding and Very Painful Thoughts

Read these penetrating words written by the apostle Peter about the prejudice and injustice Jesus endured:

> For what credit is there if, when you sin and are harshly treated, you endure it with patience? But if when you do what is right and suffer for it you patiently endure it, this finds favor with God. For you have been called for this purpose, since Christ also suffered for you, leaving you an example for you to follow in His steps, who committed no sin nor was any deceit found in His mouth; and while being reviled, He did not revile in return;

while suffering, he uttered no threats, but kept entrusting Himself to Him who judges righteously. (1 Peter 2:20–23)

I'm not a prophet. Therefore I have no way of predicting what's in store for those of us who name the name of Christ as King of kings and Lord of lords. As the debate against same-sex marriage intensifies and the battle for the family and the preservation of religious freedom escalates in this country and in other nations, I sense the church is in for some incredibly challenging days.

Already, Christians around the world are being discriminated against by those who will not tolerate a conservative faith based on Christ alone. We're in for much harder times. Countless thousands have suffered persecution, imprisonment, and even death because of their faith . . . in this generation. Prejudice against Christians is rampant, yet it largely remains under the surface. I don't believe that will be the case much longer.

When the winds of prejudice intensify, when the gale becomes of hurricane force and your faith begins to list, do not fear. Do not lose heart. Do not give up or give in. Continue to love the sinner as you stand firm against the sin. Entrust yourself to Him who judges righteously and who will help you stand alone, when necessary.

Like Christ.

❧

Quietly and gratefully, our Father, we pause before turning the page. We need to spend time reflecting on what we've just read. Don't just patch or tinker with our proud, prejudiced attitudes toward other people. Do a work of inner transformation! Refresh us with thoughts of forgiveness, acceptance, and the freedom of no longer being enslaved to the way we were taught or how our parents may have lived their lives engulfed in prejudice.

Teach us to empty ourselves as Christ emptied Himself for us. Soften our spirits, even as the Savior, who, while remaining God, became Man, and humbled Himself, and becaming obedient—even to the point of death on a Roman cross. Cause us to appreciate again the price He paid at Calvary, where He was wounded for our transgressions and crushed for our iniquities. We pray this prayer with deliberate, heart-deep surrender in the name of Jesus Christ, our Lord. Amen.

Eleven

Getting Through the Tough Stuff of Hypocrisy

TOO MANY PEOPLE LINK CHRISTIANITY with hypocrisy. One skeptic, Thomas R. Ybarra, wrote, "A Christian is a man who feels repentance on a Sunday for what he did on Saturday and is going to do on Monday."[1]

How sad, but often true.

As a boy I believed most preachers were hypocrites. A lot of them not only looked funny, they talked funny when they preached and prayed. I never could figure out why they didn't say "God" instead of "Gaaaaaawwwwd." I never understood why religious words had to be drawn out instead of simply stated.

Sadly there is a disparaging connection between clergy and hypocrisy today. The epidemic of abusive priests and swindling ministers has all but obliterated what little trust people have left in church leaders. Talk about sad!

That sort of blatant phoniness among a lot of religious leaders is nothing new. To the surprise of some, it ran rampant in Jesus's day. He constantly confronted hypocrisy among the official Jewish leaders. In fact, no fewer than seven times in one message Jesus delivered, He denounced the religious establishment by repeating the same strong rebuke, "Woe to you, scribes and Pharisees, hypocrites" (Matthew 23:13, 14, 15, 23, 25, 27, 29).

But Jesus's harsh condemnation of hypocrisy didn't end there. He railed, "Woe to you, blind guides, who say, 'Whoever swears by the temple, that is nothing; but whoever swears by the gold of the temple is obligated.' You fools and blind men! Which is more important, the gold or the temple that sanctified the gold?" (Matthew 23:16–17).

That doesn't sound like "gentle Jesus, meek and mild" to me. To look into the faces of the men who made their living allegedly serving God, exposing their gross duplicity, took remarkable courage. Chances are good you have not once this past year looked a person in the eye and called him or her a hypocrite. I openly admit, I haven't. Them's fightin' words!

What was it that got Jesus so ruffled? He loathed their self-righteous piety because "they say things and do not do them" (v. 3), and when they did do something meaningful, they did "all their deeds to be noticed by men" (v. 5). In other words, they publicly talked the talk but didn't privately walk the walk. They appeared spiritually strong but were carnal and impotent. They sounded righteous but were void of spiritual substance. Hypocrites—the whole lot of them.

If we were completely honest with ourselves, you and I would have to own up to varying degrees of hypocrisy too. We've all had to endure the tough stuff of fake faith, either when we discover it in ourselves or in someone we respect and trust. Only Jesus lived a perfectly righteous life, full of integrity and free of hypocrisy. That's why He's our model.

HYPOCRISY EXPOSED

A brief analysis of the word *hypocrisy* is in order. In Greek the word Jesus used to describe the Pharisees and their religious colleagues was *hupocritēs*. Originally and literally, the Greek term meant "one who answers back," as an orator or someone reciting poetry might do.

Theater was one of the hallmarks of Greek culture in Jesus's day. The image is one of a Greek actor playing multiple roles on stage. He disguised himself with a series of masks, which he would interchange off stage to the delight of the audience. He would come from the side of the stage with a smiling mask in front of his face as he spoke his comedy lines. The crowd would laugh uproariously over his humorous monologue, watching as the actor raced off the scene to don a frowning mask of tragic expression. With that, the actor would return and speak lines of solemn thought and sadness and, in a sense, answer back to the audience. Not surprisingly, the actor was called a "hypocrite."

Over time the word took on more negative connotations, and eventually it evolved into the word Jesus used to pinpoint the "double-masked" pretense that marked the Pharisees.

That type of pretending to be what one is not is consistently and forcefully condemned in Scripture. Every time our God takes the time to address false piety, a lack of authenticity, dissimulation, or duplicity of character, He roundly condemns it.

The Lord decried hypocrisy in His people through the mouthpiece of the ancient Hebrew prophet Isaiah.

> Because this people draw near with their words
> And honor Me with their lip service,
> But they remove their hearts far from Me,
> And their reverence for Me consists of tradition
>   learned by rote,

Therefore behold, I will once again deal marvelously with this
    people, wondrously marvelous;
And the wisdom of their wise men will perish,
And the discernment of their discerning men will be concealed.
(Isaiah 29:13–14)

Not much has changed in the several thousand years since those
words were proclaimed. I'm angered at what seems to be the unending parade of hypocrisy in organized religion today. And frankly I
don't blame unbelievers for turning off religious phonies. There is
nothing like authenticity to disarm a person without Christ. On the
other hand, nothing does more harm to the cause of Christ than
hypocritical attitudes, words, and actions modeled by people who
call themselves Christians.

New England spawned some of the most powerful preachers our
country has ever known. Some of the godliest servants of Jesus Christ
were reared and trained in the hallowed halls of such ministry training institutions as Harvard, Yale, Princeton, and Dartmouth. Those
institutions once stood strong against the swelling tide of secularism
and humanism of an emerging culture. Now, scores of the churches
and communities that built up around these universities, as well as
the seminaries they sponsored, lie in religious ruins—spiritually
hollow relics of a bygone era. In Europe the same is true. Most of the
magnificent cathedrals of Europe that once rang with faithful and
powerful gospel preaching are now virtually empty—solemn symbols
of a spiritually eroded culture.

What was at the heart of such sweeping spiritual demise?
Hypocrisy. It was a people who gave lip service to God, but whose
hearts were far from Him. Gradually people left the church to have

affairs with the world. Pulpits went silent. The gospel became muted.

It is no wonder the apostle Paul wrote to the believers in Rome with great fervor as he exhorted them to "let love be without hypocrisy" (Romans 12:9). He urged for action to match words. He desired that the phony cloaks of religious exteriors be thrown aside, exchanged for an authentic, vibrant, life-giving faith.

Peter fell into the trap of hypocrisy, as you may recall. Though he preached that all believers, both Jews and Gentiles, were one in Christ, his conduct while ministering in Antioch didn't match his words. He wore two masks—he was a *hupokritēs*—and he was exposed by Paul's stinging rebuke (Galatians 2:11–14).

Here's the point: Make sure your love is authentic. Don't be phony. Say what you mean, and mean what you say. And when you're with one group, say the same thing you said when you were with a previous group. All the while, be sure your life squares with what you say you believe. When it doesn't, admit it. Just come out and say so!

Mark Twain was reportedly once asked, "What's the difference between a liar and a person who tells the truth?" Wisely, Twain replied, "Very simple. A liar has to have a better memory." One of my favorite expressions was first said by a country preacher. "Be who you is, 'cause if you ain't who you is, you is who you ain't."

Hypocrisy occurs when we mask carnality behind a stack of religious words. That's known as being a phony. When wrestling with the tough stuff of hypocrisy, we need to listen to what Jesus said about it and allow Him to have His way in how we conduct ourselves each day. There's too much at stake to keep running on and off the stage, switching masks. It's time to let the curtain drop and end the act.

HYPOCRISY ILLUSTRATED

During His Sermon on the Mount, Jesus challenged His followers to live a life of simplicity and authenticity. He punctuated His call to genuine piety with a brief but bold exhortation: "Beware of practicing your righteousness before men to be noticed by them; otherwise you have no reward with your Father who is in heaven" (Matthew 6:1). In today's words, don't attempt to appear super-pious for the purpose of making yourself look good. Don't put on an inauthentic performance.

To the Jews in Jesus's day there were three fundamental ways of "practicing righteousness": almsgiving, praying, and fasting. Understand, Jesus never once disputes these three disciplines. His main concern was that those deeds of righteousness had become public platforms for hypocritical conduct, thanks to the modeling of the religious leaders, who hid their evil motives behind godly-looking masks. In place of that hypocritical sham Jesus gave instructions on the right way to model each of those spiritual disciplines.

First, Jesus dealt with the matter of giving.

Giving

> So when you give to the poor, do not sound a trumpet before you, as the hypocrites do in the synagogues and in the streets, so that they may be honored by men. Truly I say to you, they have their reward in full. (v. 2)

Today Jesus might tell you not to expect a big brass plate with your name on it affixed to a building because you gave a ton of money to the building fund. Don't be offended because your name doesn't appear in some public headline to honor your generosity. Don't give to make yourself look good. Jesus offers a better way: "But when you give to the poor, do not let your left hand know what your right hand is doing, so that your giving will be in secret; and your Father who sees what is done in secret will reward you" (vv. 3–4).

Give generously. Give gladly. Give sacrificially. But keep it to yourself. Your gift is nobody's business but yours and God's. And if you make it somebody's business, then you immediately have your reward. You forfeit the opportunity to receive something even greater when you arrive in heaven. God always notices and (later) rewards faithful, sacrificial giving. But when you insist on announcing it in a half-dozen pious ways, then that's all you get.

We read later in the New Testament that "God is not unjust so as to forget your work and the love which you have shown toward His name, in having ministered and in still ministering to the saints" (Hebrews 6:10). That's a promise you can trust.

Next time you're seated in church and preparing for worship, realize there are many faithful believers around you who have given and given and given again and never let it be known. You may be one of those I describe. Each Sunday you're rubbing shoulders with some of the great givers of our day. And they've done it "as unto the Lord" by keeping it to themselves and awaiting His promised reward. You will never know, but God will never forget. How good is that?

Jesus also instructs us on the right way to pray.

Praying

> When you pray, you are not to be like the hypocrites; for they love to stand and pray in the synagogues and on the street corners so that they may be seen by men. Truly I say to you, they have their reward in full. (Matthew 6:5)

In Jesus's day, the practice of prayer had degenerated in five areas that needed correcting.

First, prayer had become a formal exercise rather than a free expression. What existed were "official" prayers for all occasions. Prayers had become standardized, routine, monotonous.

Second, prayer had grown ritualistic rather than authentic in its expression. Most Jewish people prayed three times each day. The Pharisees had put in place a rigid routine of prescribed places and set times for prayer. There was no spontaneity or Spirit-initiated prayer.

Third, prayers were long and wordy. The more eloquent and flowery, the better. That was the accepted style when praying in public. My good friend Howie Hendricks coaches his seminary students to resist the temptation to pray all the way around the world and back again while leading in public prayer. "Say more by speaking less" is his frequent advice. Who wants to hear you preach a sermon when you're thanking the Lord for your sandwich? The Pharisees and religious leaders entered into those verbose petitions.

Fourth, prayers were filled with repetitions and meaningless clichés. Growing up, I had an older brother who loved Jesus long before I did. In fact, his deep and sincere faith drove me nuts. I used to wake up in the middle of the night (he had just come home from the navy and I was a teenager), and I would glance over and see the form of my brother in the moonlight silently praying on his knees. I used to think to myself, *Great Scott, why do I have to have Martin Luther for a brother? Why didn't God give me an All-American football player?* His was a vibrant, unobtrusive, living faith. Still is. Admittedly back then mine was as phony as a three-dollar bill. His authentic life was a silent rebuke.

I'll never forget the day my brother, Orville, leaned across the supper table after enduring one of my feeble memorized pre-meal petitions and asked, "Charles, when are you going to learn to pray?" At that moment, I wanted to snap back, "When are you going to learn to punt?" He knew as well as I did that my prayers were empty expressions of meaningless repetitions and clichés. And before you get too pious yourself, you might need to admit, so are some of yours. If the truth were known, a fresh prayer hasn't come from many Christians' lips in months. Jesus urges us to pray spontaneously, simply, and specifically.

Fifth, praying became a cause for pride rather than an opportunity to express humble reliance on God. William Barclay notes it had become "a legalistic status symbol to pray well. When it was followed to the letter, it led to ostentatious public display: With hands outstretched, palms upwards, and with head bowed, using eloquent words uttered loudly three times a day—preferably on a street corner."[2]

Jesus did not leave us to flounder in our struggle to overcome the tough stuff of hypocritical prayers. He talked straight:

> But you, when you pray, go into your inner room, close your door and pray to your Father who is in secret, and your Father who is in secret, and your Father who sees what is done in secret will reward you. And when you are praying, do not use meaningless repetition as the Gentiles do, for they suppose that they will be heard for their many words. (Matthew 6:6–7)

How good it is to come naturally before the Lord and talk to Him. If some of our children spoke to their dads as we talk to God, we'd laugh out loud. "Oh, great, delightful, good, and loving earthly father. What is it thou dost wish me to do?" Good grief.

By the way, this is a great place for me to insert a good word for brand-new Christians and their praying. Do you want to learn how to pray? Listen to the prayers of infant believers. They're wonderful. Spontaneous. Real. Personal. Honest. No gobbledygook. No impressive Christianese. Such straight talk that surely thrills the heart of God. They just let it all out. *I love it!*

Jesus then dealt with fasting, another discipline where hypocrisy flourished.

Fasting

> Whenever you fast, do not put on a gloomy face as the hypocrites do, for they neglect their appearance so that they will be noticed by men when they are fasting. Truly I say to you, they have their reward in full. (v. 16)

Picture the following scenario in your mind:

> The Jewish days of fasting were Monday and Thursday. These were market days, and . . . the result was that those who were ostentatiously fasting would on those days have a bigger audience to see and admire their piety. There were so many who took deliberate steps to see that others could not miss the fact that they were fasting. They walked through the streets with hair unkempt and disheveled, with clothes deliberately soiled and disarrayed. They even went the length of deliberately whitening their faces to accentuate their paleness.[3]

Showing off spiritually is blatant hypocrisy, which is precisely why Jesus warned against it. How, then, are we to fast before the Lord? Let's hear the answer from Eugene Peterson's paraphrase of Matthew 6:17–18.

When you practice some appetite-denying discipline to better concentrate on God, don't make a production out of it. It might turn you into small-time celebrity, but it won't make you a saint. If you "go into training" inwardly, act normal outwardly. Shampoo and comb your hair, brush your teeth, wash your face. God doesn't require attention-getting devices. He won't overlook what you are doing; he'll reward you well.

Embracing Tradition

Before we hang a close on the lines of this chapter, I need to mention one other area of hypocrisy Jesus confronted in the conduct of the Pharisees as well as other religious leaders. It had to do with embracing and clinging to meaningless traditions.

"Then some Pharisees and scribes came to Jesus from Jerusalem and said, 'Why do Your disciples break the tradition of the elders? For they do not wash their hands when they eat bread'" (Matthew 15:1–2). The Pharisees and scribes were first-century, card-carrying legalists. They had a rule of their own that required hand-washing before a meal. Their beef with Jesus regarding His disciples, please remember, was not a transgression of the Law of Moses but a break in the tradition of the elders.

Bible scholar Alfred Edersheim takes pains to explain the significance of this absurdity in his reputable work *The Life and Times of Jesus the Messiah*.

> Water jars were kept ready to be used before a meal. The minimum amount of water to be used was a quarter of a log, which is defined as enough to fill one and a half eggshells. The water was first poured on both hands, held with the fingers pointed

upwards, and must run up the arm as far as the wrist. It must drop off from the wrist, for the water was now itself unclean, having touched the unclean hands, and, if it ran down the fingers again, it would again render them unclean. The process was repeated with the hands held in the opposite direction, with the fingers pointing down: and then finally each hand was cleansed by being rubbed with the fist of the other. A really strict Jew would do all this, not only before a meal, but also between each of the courses.[4]

That would make anyone want to fast! Too tedious . . . too much trouble. My opinion? It would be a lot easier just to skip the meal.

Jesus immediately spotted the hypocrisy in their hearts. He wasted no words in His firm rebuke. In light of that, let yourself feel the righteous indignation Jesus experienced as He delivered His penetrating rebuke.

And He [Jesus] answered and said to them, "Why do you yourselves transgress the commandment of God for the sake of your tradition? For God said, 'Honor your father and mother' and, 'He who speaks evil of his father or mother is to be put to death.' But you say, 'Whoever says to his father or mother, "Whatever I have that would help you has been given to God," he is not to honor his father or his mother.' And by this you invalidate the word of God for the sake of your tradition. You hypocrites, rightly did Isaiah prophecy of you: 'This people honors Me with their lips, but their heart is far from Me. But in vain do they worship Me, teaching as doctrines the precepts of men.'" (Matthew 15:3–9)

The treacherous part about embracing tradition over the Scriptures is that it *invalidates* the Word of God, as Jesus put it. Never forget that. When we give people lists to live by, they'll be tempted to follow the lists more rigidly than they follow what the Bible commands. I have never seen it fail. Legalistic lists eclipse the truth as they slowly and subtly invalidate God's written word.

There's too much at stake not to counteract hypocrisy with a strategy for ridding ourselves of its toxic power. That's why we must confront hypocrisy in our churches, in our ministry training institutions, in our homes, and in those sealed-off places within our stubborn and often proud hearts.

HYPOCRISY OPPOSED AND DEFEATED

Let me offer a few practical applications to help us overcome hypocritical tendencies in ourselves or in the conduct of others.

First, exposing hypocrisy is helpful. Expose it! I urge you who are parents to address it with your children, especially those enrolled in Christian schools. They are attending what I occasionally call a religious hothouse. They are getting double doses every day of Christianity, Christianity, religion, religion, Bible, Bible, God, God, until that's virtually *all* they hear! And they could well be on their way to rebellion unless you cut it off at the pass. Maybe you haven't been told that, so let me be among the first to warn you about the subtle perils of overexposure. Without a needed balance, your children can get the wrong message and develop habits of hypocrisy that lack the authenticity of Christlikeness.

Parents, you must work hard at helping your kids take life in stride, and that includes their Christianity. We don't need another generation of uptight Christians, who do little to advance Christ's message of grace and forgiveness to an already skeptical and jaded world. Don't force prayer into everything. Don't look for a spiritual analogy in every event. Keep the home sermons to a minimum. Leave the preaching to your pastor. And please, whatever you do, don't tolerate a superficial religious veneer that they'll learn to hide behind. I have found that when that kind of religion is promoted, it leads to addictions, the worst kind of carnality, and the most unreal, unattractive Christian conduct on the planet. Until you've tried to pick up the shattered pieces of a legalistic life, you haven't witnessed the full tragedy of hypocrisy.

Second, practicing hypocrisy is natural. Resist it! Hypocritical conduct comes as naturally to Christian people as breathing. It appeals to our old nature. We get hooked on hypocrisy because it looks so impressive and results in getting lots of strokes. But in reality, it represents the ugliest underbelly of our faith, and therefore we must identify it for what it is.

Third, breaking with hypocrisy is painful. Stay at it! I'd much rather have the task of mentoring a brand-new Christian than one who's steeped in years of religion and churchy traditionalism. Still, we must stay at the process of ridding our lives, our homes, and our churches of hypocrisy's scourge. But I need to warn you, stopping hypocrisy is painful. Believe me, I know. I've got adult children (and their children) who help me try to stop it from creeping into my own life and ministry. I often tell them how much I need them to help keep me real. Truthful kids are a genuine asset!

Winning any personal battle starts with an admission of the problem. It's then that the Holy Spirit can begin a work of deliverance to put us on a path toward a genuine, permanent freedom from hypocrisy. It's a long and brutal fight.

I close with eternal words of help and hope for all of us who do battle with the tough stuff of hypocrisy—either within ourselves or being wounded by its blow from others. Overcoming hypocrisy's destructive power begins when we are completely unguarded and honest with ourselves. There's no hedging allowed, no blaming the past, no finger-pointing at someone else.

As the great apostle Paul reminds us, we have the resources of heaven on our side.

> And so I insist—and God backs me up on this—that there be no going along with the crowd, the empty-headed, mindless crowd. They've refused for so long to deal with God that they've lost touch not only with God but with reality itself. They can't think straight anymore. Feeling no pain, they let themselves go in sexual obsession, addicted to every sort of perversion.
>
> But that's no life for you. You learned Christ! My assumption is that you have paid careful attention to him, been well instructed in the truth precisely as we have it in Jesus. Since, then, we do not have the excuse of ignorance. Everything—and I do mean everything—connected with that old way of life has to go. It's rotten through and through. Get rid if it! And then take on an entirely new way of life—a God-fashioned life, a life renewed from the inside and working itself into your conduct as God accurately reproduces his character in you.
>
> What this adds up to, then, is this: no more lies, no more pretense. (Ephesians 4:17–25 MSG)

❧

Lord God, as Your Son Jesus walked this earth, He was so honest and sincere, so firm yet truly humble. But He had little patience for those who chose to fake their love for You. He openly rebuked those who were filled with themselves. Today we call them the pretenders, Lord. The incisive words of our Savior, even though spoken long, long ago, stop us in our tracks. We remember them to this moment: "Woe to you, scribes and Pharisees, hypocrites."

Oh, God, above all things, help us to be authentic people, not actors on a stage, filled with ourselves and eager for applause. Help us to be genuine to the core of our faith. Help us to admit hypocrisy in ourselves. Strengthen us to expose that which is counterfeit. Give us the courage to be honest with ourselves and to shoot straight with each other.

Grant us joy in giving privately, praying in secret, fasting quietly without crowing about it, loving the unlovable, and serving with no expectation of anything in return. And through all of these acts lived out before You, may You be the One who gets all the credit.

Through Jesus, I pray, Amen.

Twelve

Getting Through the Tough Stuff of Inadequacy

I NADEQUACY. Simply reading the word arouses an array of emotions. Very few on this earth are immune to this struggle, even those whom others think are strong and self-sufficient. Several years ago a well-known pastor's wife admitted what she and her equally well-known husband were enduring as they fought against the tough stuff of inadequacy. To protect the couple's privacy, I'll leave her words anonymous. Perhaps you can relate.

> My husband and I have occasionally felt on the edge of an ill-defined despair. Those were times when we felt a variety of things: a desire either to quit or run, a feeling of anger, the temptation to fight back at someone, the sense of being used or exploited, the weakness of inadequacy, and the reality of loneliness. Such attitudes can easily conspire to reduce the strongest and the most gifted to a state of nothingness.

Have you ever felt like that? So inadequate that you were convinced you couldn't go on? So overwhelmed you seriously considered giving up and walking away? Of course you have? *I have!* Those feelings of anger, rage, embarrassment, humiliation, fear, and loneliness that flow from a deep-seated sense of inadequacy immobilize the best of us. We often feel it most when we've been used and exploited by somebody else or when we are convinced that we simply don't measure up. At times the feelings of inadequacy run so deep we wish we could disappear.

- Inadequate to meet the needs and demands of our families
- Inadequate to fulfill the demands and expectations of our occupations, our calling
- Inadequate to perform our ministry when we feel we're in over our heads
- Inadequate to keep going in spite of the energy drain from chronic pain
- Inadequate as mothers to care every day for busy, demanding toddlers
- Inadequate to face another week when we barely made it to Sunday
- Inadequate to speak in public
- Inadequate to confront a difficult employee
- Inadequate to stop a longstanding habit or addiction
- Inadequate to learn a new job after being laid off
- Inadequate to stay in a marriage that continues to be unfulfilling
- Inadequate to take care of aging parents or all those teenagers
- Inadequate to go on living when every dream has crashed and burned

It's always something! Take it from me, even those who exude an air of confidence and poise secretly struggle with inadequacy.

Let's face it: To be human is to feel inadequate.

THE INESCAPABLE REALITY OF OUR INADEQUACY

Most people don't wake up in the morning feeling adequate and secure. That's because none of us can escape the limitations of our humanity. Maybe that's why the Bible exhorts Christians to anticipate heaven, to look for that day when we'll be glorified—fully complete in Christ and ultimately fulfilled in our heavenly home. But the fact remains that, while we remain earthbound, we will struggle with what it means to be human—to feel inadequate to handle life's demands and challenges.

What Inadequacy Means

Let's dig deeper into this pervasive plague. What does it mean to be *inadequate*? Rather than defining a negative, let me come in another door and define it positively. What does it mean to be *adequate*? To be adequate means you have sufficient ability and resources to meet a certain requirement. It means you're capable. You have what it takes to accomplish any given task or to take on any given challenge. To be inadequate then would mean just the opposite—to be incapable and without the necessary abilities or skills to complete the task. To be insufficient in who you are and limited in what you can do.

That's why most of us disguise our inadequacies. It's hard to admit to ourselves, let alone to our peers, that we are weak and incapable. Instead, we pretend we've got it all together. We act as if we are capable of handling the most challenging situations in life when, in fact, we're really not. We are basically *powerless* to face most of what we will encounter in this world. And actually there is a simple reason for that: it's the way we've been created. It's how God made us.

Why Inadequacy Exists

Few people in the Bible struggled with inadequacy to such depth as the apostle Paul. That may surprise you, but it's absolutely true. In his own words he admits that he rarely felt up to the task. As the great apostle contemplated the eternal consequences of his ministry, he struggled with intense feelings of inadequacy: "For we are a fragrance of Christ to God among those who are being saved and among those who are perishing; to the one an aroma from death to death, to the other an aroma from life to life. And who is adequate for these things?" (2 Corinthians 2:15–16).

I have felt the same struggle. Often at the end of a full day of ministry, I'll drive home with a sigh, thinking, *I'm not adequate to meet the demands of such a broad spectrum of needs.* At times the sheer weight of responsibility causes me to question my competence. Like Paul, I too ask, *Who in the world is adequate for something like this?*

Truth be told, no one is adequate—not you, not me, not even Paul. Nevertheless he enjoyed remarkable ministry success. So how did that happen? Where did he get his power? He answers that question in 2 Corinthians 3 when he writes,

> Such confidence we have through Christ toward God. Not that we are adequate in ourselves to consider anything as coming from ourselves, but our adequacy is from God, who also made us adequate as servants of a new covenant, not of the letter but of the Spirit; for the letter kills, but the Spirit gives life. (vv. 4–6)

Don't miss those five words: "our adequacy is from God." Without Him and the power He pours into us, we're incredibly anemic. Most times our weakness is in plain view. We can't cover it up.

I recall an incident I witnessed while looking through the opened blinds of a hospital room. As I looked on the parking lot below, I noticed two men attempting to get into a car. One of the men was in a wheelchair, obviously immobile. The man working with him to get him out of the chair and into the car was so patient and strong. He had to be. The older gentleman in the wheelchair was unable to move a muscle from his neck down.

At a particular point, one of the disabled man's arms dangled into the spokes of one of the wheels of the chair. With remarkable patience the caregiver gently reached down and pulled the man's limp hand out of danger. Ever so carefully, the caregiver slipped his hands behind the knees of the struggling man and then slipped his other arm behind his back. He then put his own hand under the back of the man's head and placed him in the front seat of the car. It seemed to flow like clockwork. I couldn't help thinking that this tedious ordeal had become a relentless routine for both men. With his leg, the nameless caregiver pushed against the door, leaned over and fastened the man's seatbelt, checked to make sure everything was in place, then slowly closed the door. Next, he reached down and began to fold the bulky wheelchair and lift it into the trunk.

He did *everything* for that man sitting in the car. And I'm certain, whoever he was, he's done that hundreds of times before and will do it hundreds of times again. Our tendency is to think only of the disabled person's struggle. But what I want to underscore is the energy drain on the caregiver.

Such profound physical inadequacy cannot be hidden. The disabilities the one man endured were as plainly seen as the chair that held his motionless frame. But what we tend to forget is the profound sense of inadequacy that caregiving soul must feel every day, enduring the insurmountable reality and endless tasks of caring for a loved one who cannot care for himself.

Everywhere we look we discover human inadequacy. Obviously, not all of us struggle against such severe physical weakness. But the fact is, we *are* weak—emotionally, spiritually, intellectually, and mentally. We are incapable of glorifying God in and of ourselves. We are unable to do His work our own way and in our own strength. If we are going to be His arms and His legs, His voice and His presence, it will happen only through His assistance. That's why He allows our feelings of inadequacy. *Inadequacy forces us to rely fully on God for power and strength.* I suggest you read that sentence again, only this next time, slowly and aloud. Let it sink in! That's a difficult truth for the proud and type-A assertive individual to swallow.

Not surprisingly, it's a truth Christ's disciples struggled to embrace, especially after being commissioned to span the world and proclaim God's light amid immense spiritual darkness. Can you imagine their confusion when the full load of their Christ's divine commission landed on them? Don't forget, they heard it first as Jesus was leaving the earth!

INADEQUATE FOR THE TASK GOD GIVES

Like Paul, the disciples realized how ill-equipped they were to begin a worldwide ministry. Their sense of inadequacy only intensified as they shouldered the guilt and shame of deserting Jesus. Nevertheless, after the Resurrection, Jesus commissioned them to make disciples of all nations. How could a rough-edged, unsophisticated band of followers become instruments of power to fulfill a humanly impossible mission?

A closer look at the Scriptures answers that question.

A Study in Contrasts

Following the Resurrection, the disciples met Jesus in Galilee. Matthew, one of the faithful eleven, recalls what transpired when he writes, "The eleven disciples proceeded to Galilee, to the mountain which Jesus had designated. When they saw Him, they worshiped Him; but some were doubtful" (Matthew 28:16–17).

Think of the contrasts between Jesus and His disciples. On the one hand, you have eleven trembling, confused, and doubting disciples. On the other hand stands the all-powerful, completely adequate, risen Lord. They were human—limited, weak, feeble, frail, and prone to failure. He was God's promised Messiah, fully human and fully divine, omniscient, omnipotent, omnipresent, all-sufficient deity.

Among the group was Peter, who had deliberately denied Jesus, a former tax collector, and a couple of hot-tempered fishermen from Galilee. They had only witnessed miracles Jesus had performed. The disciples feared the raging storm on the Sea of Galilee. Jesus commanded the wind and the waves to be still. The disciples ran for their lives out of the Garden of Gethsemane. Jesus faced His death with undaunted resolve.

I don't want to give the impression that the disciples were subpar in intelligence or that they were low on zeal or devotion. They were just human—devoted and willing, but unquestionably *inadequate*.

All of that was about to change.

A Command and a Promise

Before we look down our noses at the disciples, let's admit we may have been doubtful too. Their hopes had been dashed as their Master breathed His last on that cruel cross. The whole mystery of Jesus's bodily, miraculous resurrection had yet to work itself out in their confused minds. Uncertainties lingered . . . some were small and fleeting, others more significant and haunting. They were swamped with questions. Christ's plan for them would provide not only clear answers to their questions but the needed solution to their inadequacies.

Matthew continues,

> And Jesus came up and spoke to them, saying, "All authority has been given to Me in heaven and on earth. Go therefore and make disciples of all the nations, baptizing them in the name of the Father and the Son and the Holy Spirit, teaching them to observe all that I commanded you; and lo I am with you always, even to the end of the age." (Matthew 28:18–20)

Jesus had given the disciples a command to "make disciples of all the nations." But to do that they had to leave the comfort and ease of their own surroundings. They had to forsake everything to obey Him. They must have buckled under the weight of such a mammoth assignment. How could they possibly accomplish all that He expected of them (especially since He would soon be gone)? They were not equipped to perform miracles as Jesus was. They could not read the hearts and thoughts of men as He could. Sure, He had promised never to leave them and to grant to them His own heavenly authority. But would that be enough? They needed more than a command and a promise. They needed power—*His* power! Somehow there would have to be a transfer of His power to each one of them. No one knew that better than Jesus.

HIS POWER MADE PERFECT IN WEAKNESS

Luke, the writer of the New Testament book of Acts, picks up where the Gospels leave off—following the Resurrection and before

Christ's ascension to heaven. Read Luke's words slowly and thoughtfully, as if you're encountering them for the first time. As you do, remember the disciples had just received their commission and were likely fighting off debilitating feelings of personal and collective inadequacy!

> Gathering them together, He commanded them not to leave Jerusalem, but to wait for what the Father had promised, "Which," He said, "you heard of from Me; for John baptized with water, but you will be baptized with the Holy Spirit not many days from now. . . . But you will receive power when the Holy Spirit has come upon you; and you shall be My witnesses both in Jerusalem, and in all Judea and Samaria, and even to the remotest part of the earth." (Acts 1:4–5, 8)

Earlier, Jesus had told the disciples of such power. He had explained how the Holy Spirit would come and empower them. That took place while they were together with Jesus in the Upper Room in a home somewhere in Jerusalem (John 13–16). It was there Jesus spoke to them about a transfer of authority—a deposit of power within them, which would overcome their weakness and enable them to carry out the commission.

Jesus was asking the impossible of the tiny band of reluctant evangelists. But that was precisely the point. They needed *His* power to accomplish *His* command. They needed to be *transformed.* May I remind you? So do we!

All the hoping and dreaming in the world won't make it possible for me to sit down at a piano and play a Beethoven sonata like Van Cliburn. Nice idea but an impossible notion. But if the world-renowned pianist were somehow able to confer on me all the skill and brilliance of his ability, undergirded by his decades of study and practice and magnificent talent, perhaps I could pull it off. But make no mistake, that would require a transfer of Van Cliburn's musical genius into my very being. I would need his spirit within me, literally.

That's what we face in the Christian life. Christ has given us His power through the infilling presence of the Holy Spirit. The Holy Spirit indwells us when we turn to God through faith in His Son. No need to pray, dance, hope, shout, or plead for divine power. If you are a follower of Christ, you *have* Christ's power in you. The Holy Spirit literally resides within your being. The more you yield your life to Him, the more His power flows through you. He is there, ready and able to empower us. Is that great news or what?

Now back to the first century. The disciples were to wait in Jerusalem for the Spirit's power to descend on them. It would be the very same power they saw at work in Jesus's miraculous life. It would be a power strong enough to transform these men filled with inadequacy, limitations, and fear into bold, courageous, and capable witnesses for Christ. Talk about *transformed!*

In his classic work *The Training of the Twelve,* New Testament authority A. B. Bruce writes,

> All that the apostles were to gain from the mission of the Comforter—enlightenment of mind, enlargement of heart, sanctification of their faculties, and transformation of their characters, so as to make them whetted swords . . . for subduing the world unto truth; these, or the effect of these combined, constituted the power for which Jesus directed the eleven to wait.
>
> . . . It was evidently indispensable to success.
>
> . . . The world is to be evangelized, not by men invested in ecclesiastical dignities and with party-colored garments, but by men who have experienced the baptism of the Holy Spirit, and

who are visibly endued with the divine power of wisdom, and love, and zeal.

As the promised power was indispensable, so it was in its nature a thing simply to be waited for. The disciples were directed to tarry till it came. They were neither to attempt to do without it. . . . They fully understood that the power was needful, and that it could not be got up, but must come down.[1]

And indeed, the power came down. Acts 2 records the amazing event when the Spirit came as promised; the disciples were completely transformed, and the church was born. Were the disciples still men—mere humans? Yes. But deep within their being there came an empowering enablement that resulted in their turning the world upside down.

POWER IN PLACE OF INADEQUACY

I want to reserve my concluding thoughts for anyone who is willing to meet Christ in the tough stuff of inadequacy. Hopefully that includes you. However long you've felt the way you do and however deep your despair, the answer to your need is a Person, whose name is Jesus. He alone has the power you need that can counteract your weakness. Remember, Jesus died for your sin *and* for your inadequacies.

Here are a couple of simple principles you can put into place to apply His power to your inadequacy.

First, admit your inadequacies. This is the initial step toward accepting God's power. I've never known anyone to overcome the struggle of a deep, debilitating sense of inadequacy without first acknowledging his or her need for God's help. That's true of drug addicts, sex addicts, alcoholics, gamblers, spouse abusers, hotheads, procrastinators, perfectionists, fretters, worriers, the impatient, the fearful, the depressed, the disobedient, even the dying. The category of your weakness does not matter. As a matter of fact, the more impossible to overcome the better. That's when you and I are most likely to acknowledge our desperate need for God's power.

If you're too proud to admit your need, you'll remain powerless in your inadequacy. It's that simple. The apostle Paul knew the power that lay in weakness and humbly admitted his need for God's power.

> And when I came to you, brethren, I did not come with superiority of speech or of wisdom, proclaiming to you the testimony of God. For I determined to know nothing among you except Jesus Christ, and Him crucified. I was with you in weakness and in fear and in much trembling, and my message and my preaching were not in persuasive words of wisdom, but in demonstration of the Spirit and of power. (1 Corinthians 2:1–4)

> But we have this treasure in earthen vessels, so that the surpassing greatness of the power will be of God and not from ourselves. (2 Corinthians 4:7)

Listen to Paul's personal story. This explains how he acknowledged his inadequacy and found it to be God's way of using him even more effectively because of it.

> I was given the gift of a handicap to keep me in constant touch with my limitations. Satan's angel did his best to get me down; what he in fact did was push me to my knees. No danger then of walking around high and mighty! At first I didn't think of it as a gift, and begged God to remove it. Three times I did that, then he told me.

"My grace is enough; it's all you need.
My strength comes into its own in your weakness."

Once I heard that, I was glad to let it happen. I quit focusing on the handicap and began appreciating the gift. It was a case of Christ's strength moving in on my weakness. Now I take limitations in stride, and with good cheer, these limitations that cut me down to size—abuse, accidents, opposition, bad breaks. I just let Christ take over! And so the weaker I get, the stronger I become. (2 Corinthians 12:7–10 MSG)

If the apostle Paul were to be resurrected today and ushered through St. Paul's Cathedral in London, he would shudder in embarrassment. He would never have approved of such an elaborate structure to be built in his honor. All the way to his death, Paul remained one of the most self-effacing and self-denying servants the church has ever known. He understood the power of weakness like few before him and fewer since. I don't care how long you may have walked with the Savior, how big your church is, or how much you give to the ministry; *every ounce of your adequacy comes from God, not from yourself.* After admitting that, may we never forget it!

Second, claim Christ's power. This is the ultimate secret to living above the drag of humanity. I want to take you back to a very difficult period in my own life. It was back in the mid-1960s. I'll spare you the details of the situation, but you need to know I had come to the lowest point of my adult life. I was confused about what I needed to do. Bewildered by God's silence, I was frustrated with my circumstances. I felt completely alone in my struggle. Inadequacy had me by the throat, and I was choking in its grip. I absolutely did not know what to do, who to talk to, or how I could go on. I felt absolutely at the end of my rope.

I remember walking out the back door of our home and down the driveway that led to an alley that ran the whole distance of the block. All alone, sobbing audibly, I took a long walk under the moonlight. I told God *everything*. I held nothing back. My sobbing intensified. Suddenly all the fear and pain and anguish erupted from my heart in a rush of emotion. I stopped walking and I looked up at the moon. I then deliberately released to God the heaviness of that burden I had been carrying for so long. I had enjoyed a fair measure of success, both in seminary and in my first year or two of ministry, but the test I was in would not let up. In fact, it was getting worse. No one on earth knew the ache of my soul. Others saw me as strong, but I was crushed by feelings of weakness. Others would have considered me secure, but I wasn't.

Alone in the dark, in that back alley somewhere behind my house, I knelt down and acknowledged my inadequacies to God. I then claimed His all-sufficient power. In the next few seconds I felt like a half-ton of weight was lifted off my shoulders. I stood up, the sobbing stopped, and there was a transformation that came over me as I walked back home.

I've never looked back. Sure, I've had my relapses of fear and doubting, but I will never forget the moment I relinquished everything to God and felt His power take control.

When I got to the back porch of our home, I felt an incredible sense of relief. To this day I can remember it, though it occurred over four decades ago. A surge of strength returned. Only Jesus could transform my weakness into strength. A quiet confidence overwhelmed me. Only Jesus could transfer my inadequacy into confidence. And He can do it for you too. I urge you to let Him!

Haven't you lived your life long enough strapped down by inadequacy and self-doubt? Aren't you weary of the struggle of always feeling that you don't belong? Won't you admit it—now? Good. That's precisely where Christ wants you. At the bottom. At the end of your rope. At the end of yourself.

That's where He can do His best work—in your weakness. That's His plan. He doesn't use superstrong, self-assertive, self-centered people. He uses weak, trembling, inadequate, ill-equipped people—people just like you and like me.

If you have retreated to the back alley of life and are wallowing in all your inadequacies, then you're exactly where God needs you to be to demonstrate His power. It's time to kneel humbly before Him and let go. Release your grip. Pour out your heart.

You have a Savior who is waiting to demonstrate His great power in you. Don't waste another minute trying to get through the tough stuff of inadequacy on your own. Don't run *away* from this test. Run *to* Him and receive His power.

As Paul put it, I suggest you "quit focusing on the handicap and begin appreciating the gift." Let Christ take over.

Now.

Thirteen

Getting Through the Tough Stuff of Disqualification

FOR MANY YEARS A.W. Tozer wrote like a prophet to a spiritually barren people. These are some of the sobering words he penned about the perils of being disqualified.

> The ministry is one of the most perilous of professions. The devil hates the Spirit-filled minister with an intensity second only to that which he feels for Christ Himself. The source of this hatred is not difficult to discover. An effective, Christlike minister is a constant embarrassment to the devil, a threat to his dominion, a rebuttal of his best arguments and a dogged reminder of his coming overthrow. No wonder he hates him.
>
> Satan knows that the downfall of a prophet of God is a strategic victory for him, so he rests not day or night devising hidden snares and deadfalls for the ministry. Perhaps a better

figure would be the poison dart that only paralyzes its victim, for I think that Satan has little interest in killing the preacher outright. An ineffective, half-alive minister is better advertisement for hell than a good man dead. . . .

There are indeed some very real dangers of the grosser sort which the minister must guard against, such as love of money and women; but the deadliest perils are far more subtle than these.[1]

Though Tozer's words are targeted specifically to ministers, they relate to all believers who name the name of Christ. The perils we face are just as subtle. All of us must be on guard against the devil's insidious schemes.

In fact, this a good place for me to insert some thoughts on a particularly troubling trend, which I mentioned in chapter 1. My thoughts return to the perils of Internet pornography.

Dread fills our hearts when we hear that another young girl has disappeared. We see her image smiling at us from the television screen, or we read about her in the newspapers, and we wonder immediately whether she's been raped and killed. That is so often the case, and in the great majority of these tragedies the guilty party was involved in some type of pornography. Sadly that is the reality of our world today.

As Christians we have generally felt we were immune from the evils of our society—that the body of Christ was insulated from the darkest sins committed by those who belonged to the world. But today there is an evil that has slithered its way into the very heart of our churches and families. That evil, I repeat, is Internet pornography.

By now you have surely heard the statistics. One in every two churchgoers is actively involved with Internet porn. Nine out of ten children between the ages of eight and sixteen have been exposed to

Internet pornography—most of them accidentally, while doing their homework online. And a full 37 percent of pastors say that Internet porn is a current struggle in their lives. Most are exposed through unexpected computer screen pop-ups, unsolicited e-mail, or through links to Web sites with innocent-sounding names. And when an enticing image flashes, the temptation is hard to overcome, especially for males.

The Internet has become an integral part of our lives. We all know there is much about it that is good, but there is just as much that is deadly. It is therefore our responsibility as Christians to protect ourselves from the dangers that are a part of Internet usage. Here is one way we can do it.

BsafeOnline is the world's best Internet filter software for the Christian family, and I highly recommend it to you. Bsafe is a software product, not an Internet service provider. Thus it works alongside your current provider (such as AOL), and your Internet speed will *not* be affected. It is customizable—it can be set up according to your personal needs. Plus, it is updated *daily,* so there are no manual updates needed. Check out www.bsafeonline.com.

I believe so strongly in this product that I encourage every Christian family to take advantage of its protection. Actually I believe Bsafe should be installed in churches, schools, offices, and wherever a computer is used by Christian people.

As Christians, we are accountable to the Lord and to those we love. Deuteronomy 22:8 says, "When you build a new house, you shall make a parapet for your roof so that you will not bring blood-guilt on your house if anyone falls from it."

We need to build a parapet (or wall) around our Internet usage to guard against falling into the bottomless pit of depravity that is present on the Internet. Bsafe can be that wall.

Bsafe also provides another solution I mentioned earlier. It is called

NetAccountability. With this feature a report of your Internet activity can be forwarded on a weekly basis to as many as three individuals to whom you want to be accountable for your Internet usage. In this report, your "accountability partners" will be sent regular reports that detail both where you've been on the Internet and how long you stayed there. This will provide an opportunity for regular communication with your partner holding you accountable for all your Internet activities. NetAccountability (www.netaccountability.com) is excellent for those struggling to overcome the temptations of Internet pornography.

Bsafe is, in my opinion one of the most effective Internet filter software products on the market. Yet the management of Bsafe is well aware that technology is not the real answer to Internet pornography—that a change of heart through Jesus Christ is the only real answer. But Bsafe provides a safe, reliable way for believers to avoid the onslaught of temptation that comes with the use of the Internet.

I believe that removing Internet pornography use from the body of Christ is a winnable battle that will eventually come through repentance and prayer and daily time in the Word. Other vital weapons in this battle include accountability and avoidance of the temptations that lure us into sin. Bsafe provides these last two weapons. I hope you'll strap them on.

You can do so by going to Insight for Living's Web site at www.insight.org. Here you will be given instructions for going to BsafeOnline's Web site where you can easily install this software on your computer. Bsafe's software will prevent even accidental exposure to pornography from advertisements. As I mentioned in chapter 1, it is estimated that twenty-five hundred new pornography sites are introduced to the Internet every week. Their marketing strategy is to have you accidentally exposed to their sites through clever marketing schemes. This explains how young children have become addicted to pornography as early as eight years of age, and they feed that addiction in the middle of the night when parents are sleeping. It is therefore compelling that all parents should consider this small investment for the protection of their children. Needless to say, since most porn sites are visited by teenagers and adults, this protection is needed by everyone, especially those who are in a constant battle for moral purity.

A CULTURE WITHOUT FEAR

Frankly I am concerned today about the absence of fear among God's people, which makes us extremely vulnerable to the subtle dangers I referred to above. I'm not intending to instill fright, but a respectful, healthy fear of the Lord. This would include an acknowledgment of the fact that there are both good and bad consequences to our actions and that we are accountable. Being proactive is essential if we hope to walk in purity.

Sadly, many Christians live carelessly. Our shallow culture does not promote a wholesome fear of disqualification. That's perilous! Those who live with such slipshod disregard risk bringing shame to their Master and dance dangerously near the edge of disqualifying themselves from service. When a minister falls morally, the impact tends to be more scandalous. Certainly the congregation he serves suffers. His immediate family feels the wounds even more deeply. Furthermore the community in which he serves is dealt a damaging blow. But whenever any Christian falls into sin, the witness of the gospel is diminished, if not silenced altogether. That's why getting through the tough stuff of disqualification is so critical—because there's so much at stake. God's Word provides a clear picture of the righteous standard Christians must uphold. And it also reveals the devastating consequences that occur when we don't.

SCRIPTURAL WORD PICTURES OF A LIFE WELL LIVED

We looked closely at the subject of hypocrisy in chapter 11. In doing so we discovered that Christ's perspective on hypocritical people was straightforward. He said it all in five single-syllable words: "Do not be like them" (Matthew 6:8). Unless we are unlike those who live as if God does not exist, we run the risk of being disqualified. That's why He was so severe in His condemnation of the Pharisees. So what are we to be like?

As Salt and Light

Read slowly and thoughtfully the words of Jesus recorded in Matthew 5, a portion of Scripture referred to as the Sermon on the Mount.

> You are the salt of the earth; but if the salt has become tasteless, how can it be made salty again? It is no longer good for anything, except to be thrown out and trampled under foot by men.
>
> You are the light of the world. A city set on a hill cannot be hidden; nor does anyone light a lamp and put it under a basket, but on the lampstand, and it gives light to all who are in the house. Let your light so shine before men in such a way that they may see your good works, and glorify your Father who is in heaven. (vv. 13–16)

We are to be the kind of people who create a thirst for God in others. We are to make them thirsty for things eternal. That's what Christ means by being *salt*. Salt has a preserving quality. Without salt, food becomes tasteless . . . ultimately, useless.

Jesus also underscored the importance of our being reflectors of God's enduring light. The way we live dispels the spiritual darkness that pervades this chaotic world. Like burning candles, Christians light up the world with the shining rays of Christ's grace and love. Tragically the world is full of lamps that once burned brightly but have gone out. The salt is void of its savor. Each one of us can make a difference by living rightly in "the midst of a crooked and perverse generation" (Philippians 2:15).

Besides being salt and light, Paul provides another vivid word picture of how we are to live.

As a Well-Trained Athlete

Successful athletes are not born; they're deliberately cultivated. In 1 Corinthians 9, Paul provides a mental picture worth considering. It's the picture of one who disciplines and develops his body and mind in order to lead an effective Christian life: "Do you not know that those who run in a race all run, but only one receives the prize? Run in such a way that you may win. Everyone who competes in the games exercises self-control in all things. They then do it to receive a perishable wreath, but we an imperishable" (vv. 24–25). I appreciate the insight one author provides on this compelling theme.

> [Paul] insists to those Corinthians who wanted to take the easy way that no man will ever get anywhere without the sternest self-discipline. Paul was always fascinated by the picture of the athlete. An athlete must train with intensity if he is to win his contest; and Corinth knew how thrilling contests could be, for at Corinth the Isthmian games, second only to the Olympic games, were held. Furthermore, the athlete undergoes this self-discipline

and this training to win a crown of laurel leaves that within days will be withered chaplet. How much more should the Christian discipline himself to win the crown which is eternal life? [2]

Paul had an imperishable, eternal crown in mind, one that will never lose its luster. He also knew such rewards were not given automatically. What is required of all who desire it is a life of rigorous spiritual training as they compete in the game in order to win the prize. That explains why he writes, "Therefore, I run in such a way, as not without aim; I box in such a way, as not beating the air; but I discipline my body and make it my slave, so that, after I have preached to others, I myself will *not be disqualified*" (vv. 26–27, italics added). Paul anticipated winning the prize, but he understood the sacrifice that was required to receive it: A life well-lived, free from behaviors and attitudes that would disqualify him.

Something that important deserves a great deal of attention.

WHEN DISQUALIFICATION BECOMES PERSONAL

What does it mean to be *disqualified?* As New Testament scholar and former Dean of Canterbury, Henry Alford, explains, "An examination of the victorious combatants took place after the contest, and if it could be proved that they had contended unlawfully, or unfairly, they were deprived of the prize and driven with disgrace from the games." [3]

The Greek word Paul uses for "disqualified" is *adokimos*. In Paul's day, and especially in ancient Greek culture, there were few things more shameful for a community to endure than to have their star athlete *adokimos*—disqualified from competition.

You don't hear much about that in our day of prima donna athletes. Few athletes are absolutely and permanently disqualified.

Only scant evidence of such high standards remains even in our military system. I recall many years ago while I was a Marine watching as men lost the right to bear their rank. They would stand before their commanding officers and endure the humiliation of having their chevrons stripped from their sleeves to be left partially hanging in shreds. I've seen gunnery sergeants and master sergeants stripped of their rank and disgraced in front of their companies. I've watched in anguish as officers performed that solemn duty with tears of regret and sadness. It's horrible to be publicly disqualified . . . it's equally horrible to witness it.

Of course, I'm not referring here to our Olympic games or the American military. I'm attempting to point out the enormous responsibility, the high privilege of bearing the message of the Savior. Then because of careless, irresponsible living to have it all stripped away. Admittedly, some are not as exacting as I. Nevertheless I would challenge anyone to find in Scripture a place that offers a quick and painless transition from disqualification back to a significant rank in ministry. There are times I feel like a voice in the wilderness holding to these deep convictions. But I'm convinced there is the very real possibility of *disqualification*.

Let me be clear: If you know Christ as Savior and Lord, you cannot lose your hope of heaven or the guaranteed promise of His forgiving grace. Yours is an eternal salvation once you've trusted in Christ by faith. Our God is full of grace and faithful to forgive.

What you can lose is the magnificent privilege and blessing of serving Him publicly and in significant places of ministry. And let this word go out to all Bible colleges, seminaries, and ministry training institutions: guard what you have been given in the influencing of young men and women called to proclaim the gospel. Exhort them to develop a deep passion for the Word, an unswerving devotion to the church, and an unrelenting pursuit of holiness and purity in their personal lives and public ministries. Every new generation must be challenged to hold the standard high!

Developing and maintaining a healthy fear of the Lord is for all Christians, especially those entering the ministry. That explains why we take our official ordination so seriously. The respect we receive from those we serve depends on it. Little boys and girls can then with confidence fix their eyes on their senior pastor or youth pastor or Sunday school leader as a model and say, "There's at least one person I know who is true to his or her word. I can trust that person." How I long for that to be restored in our great land. My heart grieves every time I hear the account of another fall.

Now, it's our tendency to think that dangers come as a result of our being part of a sinful world. That's only partly true. The secret is in setting personal boundaries. If anyone maintained proper boundaries of protection against the allure of the world, it was Paul. He wasn't contaminated by the system. His entire life was committed to pursuing spiritual things. He loved the Lord. Like Christ, he stands to this day as an excellent model of godly living. Yet, even Paul in all his zeal and lifelong devotion to Christ, was at risk from exposure to spiritual things. You and I both know how overexposure to spiritual truth can breed a dangerous indifference and taking for granted things that matter. How easy it is to develop a perfunctory spirit in the performance of spiritually significant activities!

Silent Perils of Overexposure

Perhaps Paul had a flash of insight when we he was writing these warnings to the Corinthian believers. An illustration from the Old Testament came to him as a fitting picture of the perils of overexposure. He wrote of the people of Israel taking in the glory of God's goodness and provision while neglecting the attitudes of their hearts.

> For I do not want you to be unaware, brethren, that our fathers were all under the cloud and all passed through the sea; and all were baptized into Moses in the cloud and in the sea; and all ate the same spiritual food; and all drank the same spiritual drink, for they were drinking from a spiritual rock which followed them; and the rock was Christ. (1 Corinthians 10:1–4)

You get the picture. The Israelites had it made as they lived under God's generous provisions and sheltering cloud. They had everything they needed. God led them through the Exodus. He was there throughout their journey to the Promised Land. Surely they were the personification of faithful followers. Surely they carried out their responsibility to live holy lives. *Not!* Paul writes, "Nevertheless, with most of them God was not well-pleased; for they were laid low in the wilderness" (v. 5).

Had you lived as a Hebrew in that generation when Moses stood against Pharaoh, you would have known your standing before God. You would have realized that you were one of God's chosen people—Jews who witnessed the Exodus! It's a marvelous group among whom to be numbered.

What would you have experienced? You would have been "under the cloud," enjoying *supernatural guidance.* You would have been among those who "passed through the sea," thereby experiencing *supernatural deliverance.* Imagine being a part of that mind-boggling event.

You would have gloried in the blessings of being a part of Moses's flock—benefiting from his remarkable giftedness and *supernatural leadership.* You lacked nothing. You had unlimited supplies of food and water, never a worry about a place to stay, no fear of losing your way in the rugged wilderness expanse. None of that. Surely the Jews must have been a faithful and grateful people.

Not on your life! They were everything but that. They had grown fat and complacent, overexposed to the blessings of God's goodness. In Paul's words, God disqualified the whole lot of them.

Just like well-coached and highly gifted athletes can drift into drugs and get out of shape, becoming washouts, so can we, who know and enjoy the blessings of God, wind up awash. We too can be disqualified. Gifted, capable, competent people are easy prey for the predators of disqualification. Too much of a good thing makes us vulnerable. Overexposed, we can become indifferent, lazy, carnal, discontented, and ultimately out of touch.

Let's remember, Paul's words were not preserved on the pages of Scripture simply for the benefit of historians. In somber tones Paul drives home his major concern, reminding us that "these things happened to them as an example, and they were written for our instruction, upon whom the ends of the ages have come" (v.11). As Eugene Peterson paraphrases it in *The Message*, "These are all warning markers—DANGER!—in our history books, written down so that we don't repeat their mistakes."

The Greek word translated "example" is *tupos*, which literally means "to strike a blow," like the stamp of a die that leaves a permanent impression. The impression remains on the mind to be a continual reminder of the cost of rebelling against God.

Let's remember A.W. Tozer's words: "The deadliest influences are the subtle ones."

Subtle Temptations of Cynicism

Look back to verse 6 of 1 Corinthians 10. Paul writes that "these things happened, as examples for us so that we would not crave evil things as they also craved." Drifting starts with craving evil things. Plain and simple, the battle begins in the mind and heart. Things of the world become curiously exciting. Those shameful secret thoughts and silent temptations! They come at the most inappropriate times. Left unchecked, they grow and become more lurid until eventually they possess us. Before we realize it, it's too late. It's over and we're disqualified.

It happens in much the same way an Eskimo hunts and kills a wolf. If these words don't register with you, I'm not sure what will. Read them slowly and thoughtfully. They are not pleasant. The account is grisly, yet it offers fresh insight into the consuming, self-destructive nature of sin.

First, the Eskimo coats his knife blade with animal blood and allows it to freeze. Then he adds another layer of blood, and another, until the blade is completely concealed by frozen blood. Next, the hunter pushes the handle of his knife in the snow, blade up. When a wolf follows its sensitive nose to the source of the scent and discovers the bait, it begins to lick it, tasting the fresh frozen blood. The licking accelerates and intensifies, as the wolf more and more vigorously laps against the blade until the keen edge is bare. Feverishly then, harder and harder the wolf licks the blade long into the arctic night. So great becomes its craving for blood that the wolf does not notice the razor-sharp sting of the naked blade on its own tongue, nor does the animal recognize the instant at which its insatiable thirst is being satisfied by its own warm blood. The carnivorous appetite of the wild wolf just craves more—until the dawn finds it dead in the blood-soaked snow.

Disqualification follows the same pattern. We are consumed by our own sinful desires until we find ourselves out of control, addicted, trapped by our own appetite for more. It begins with a secret craving of evil things. It may be with another person. It could be Internet pornography or a half-dozen other types of temptation—all of them designed to disqualify you. I challenge anyone secretly craving and cultivating the beginning of an addiction to *stop now* before it's too late. Get help immediately. If you're becoming addicted to prescription drugs or alcohol or food or whatever, confess your struggle to someone you trust. Do whatever it takes to face your addiction, to confess it, to come to terms with it.

Countless individuals who triumphantly marched out of Egypt under the mighty hand of God drifted far from their earlier devotion. Ultimately, they died miserable, horrible deaths in the wilderness. It's as if Paul were writing to you and me when he warns, "Do not be idolaters, as some of them were; as it is written, 'the people sat down to eat and drink, and stood up to play.' Nor let us act immorally, as some of them did, and twenty-three thousand fell in one day" (1 Corinthians 10:7–8).

Idolatry occurs, in simplest terms, when we put something else in place of Christ. It can happen by means of a silent, often secret, dethroning of Christ in our lives. Idolatry happens when we are habitually preoccupied with something or someone other than Christ. Like beach erosion, it makes no noise and attracts no attention, but ends in obvious destruction. Allowed to continue, everything is washed away. *Everything.*

From idolatry we move to the point where we mentally shake our fists at God. In Paul's words we "try the Lord" (v. 9). This is the sin of presumption—taking willful advantage of God's grace, presuming on His longsuffering, as we dance near the edge of disaster.

From there it deteriorates further still. From idolatry to presumption, to *grumbling against God* (v. 10). What a pitiful scene that must have been! God's people, who had enjoyed His glorious provisions, grumbled and whined in the desert.

Paul wasn't talking about pagan, reprobate souls who never knew God or embraced His claims. We might expect such from unbelievers. No. He was delivering his warning to Christians who had experienced God's best. And in the hothouse of their self-centered world, it went sour.

Every moral fall has a history. There is no such thing as a "spiritual blowout" in the Christian life. It all begins with a series of small, imperceptible leaks in the linings of our character. Though the final and deliberate act of the fall may be sudden and disastrous, it has a long, lingering, lurid past. Through rationalization, the salt loses its bite, and our light begins to flicker. We diminish the truth with our compromise. It can happen to me. It can happen to you. It can happen to your best friend . . . your mate . . . your own child. Thankfully there is a path that leads us back to God's tender mercies. I am pleased to tell you, God awaits with open arms the return of any prodigal.

RESPONDING TO DEFEAT GOD'S WAY

Paul realized his readers would respond in one of two ways. Some will say, "This would never happen to me." For them he warned, "Let him who thinks he stands take heed that he does not fall" (1 Corinthians 10:12). In other words, no one is immune. Anyone can fall. Therefore we need to heed every warning the Scripture provides. I repeat, we are *all* in peril of being disqualified. There is no such thing as a perpetual promise of purity. Hope and forgiveness, yes . . . purity and effectiveness, no.

And then others will say, "I'm in so deep I can never get out. The mess I've made of my life is too great for me ever to hope for recovery. It's too late for me." To these people Paul wrote, "No temptation has overtaken you but such as is common to man; and *God is faithful,* who will not allow you to be tempted beyond what you are able, but with the temptation will provide the way of escape also, so that you will be able to endure it" (1 Corinthians 10:13).

Isn't that magnificent news? God not only knows your struggle, He promises you a way to escape it. To get beyond it. He will help you escape from your imprisoned condition. What a gracious, compassionate, merciful God!

Getting Back in the Race

This has been one of the more challenging chapters to write, because helping people through the tough stuff of disqualification is a sobering, painful process. I cannot number the times I have been involved in restoring those who have fallen. These are extremely difficult truths to present and to apply, but they are essential if we are to stay in the race . . . and win the prize.

By the way, this is not something for just your neighbor to read. This is not something just for your minister or your husband. This is for you, yes *you* . . . man or woman, young or old, in the church or far from the church, married or widowed or divorced.

I have several Bibles. One is especially important and meaningful to me. It is a copy of the New Testament I received shortly after graduating from seminary. It is well worn, marked up, and coming apart. I still use it on occasion (though sometimes two or three pages drop out and I have to catch them!). When I first got it, I was young in the ministry. So, to warn myself of the dangers I'd be facing in the years ahead, I pasted on the inside cover the words of Charles Haddon Spurgeon, a British pastor God used so effectively back in the nineteenth century. Spurgeon's warning, though old and quaintly worded, is as relevant as anything written today. There are times I stop and reread these words. I remind myself that anyone can fall . . . including *me*.

The first thing we are to consider is *our danger*. We are in danger of falling—not only some of us, but all of us; not merely the weak, but also the strong; not the young alone, but the old and middle-aged, all are in danger of falling into sin, and so bringing dishonour upon our profession, sorrow to our own souls, and disgrace upon the name of Christ, whom we profess to love and serve.

That we are in danger, should strike us very clearly, because we have seen others fall into sin. I scarcely dare to recall all that I have seen during my observation of the professing church of Christ. Though I think I have been peculiarly favoured as a pastor, there are sore places in my soul—bleeding wounds that never will be healed this side of heaven, that have been caused by the backsliding of men with whom I took sweet counsel, and in whose company I used to walk to the house of God. I have known some, who have preached the gospel and preached it with power, but live to depart from it altogether. I have known others, who have served at the Lord's table, who have discharged the duties of the deaconship or eldership with considerable diligence, who have afterwards given way to their evil passions. I have thought some of them to be amongst the holiest of men. While they have been praying, I have been lifted up in devotion to the very gates of heaven; and if anyone had said to me that they would one day fall into gross sin, I could not have believed it. I would sooner have believed it to be possible of myself.

Those who seemed stronger than we are have fallen, so why

may not we? Nay, shall we not fall unless sovereign grace shall prevent that dread calamity? Our Lord's disciples, who sat at the table with him, when they were told that one of them would betray their Master, each one enquired, "Lord, is it I?" That was a very proper question. There was not one who asked, "Lord, is it Judas?" Probably, no one of them even suspected him, and it may be that the worst hypocrite in this assembly is the one upon whom there does not rest, at this moment, a single shade of suspicion. He has learnt to play his part so well that his true character has not yet been discovered.[4]

Many win. Sadly, many others lose. Samson ultimately lost; David ultimately won. Both suffered disqualifying events in their leadership. Yet the difference came in their response.

Samson served as a judge over Israel for twenty years. His two weak spots, however, were pride and sex. Once used mightily by God, Samson gave in to his lustful and proud ways. He got involved with a prostitute and then fell in love with another woman named Delilah (Judges 16). Eventually he wound up literally in the lap of that deceptive woman in the Valley of Sorek. Philistine country. Enemy territory. His pride-born sexual exploits culminated in a humiliating, manipulative affair, by which he not only lost his hair— a symbol of enduring strength—but also the power and favor of God. He lay powerless and defeated. Struck down.

Disqualified.

Samson went too far. He wound up in humiliating defeat, his eyes gouged out, mocked by his captors in a Philistine dungeon.

David also lived a life of passion. He struggled against the unrelenting temptation to live by his own remarkable talents and abilities. He, too, in a moment of weakness, let down his guard and fell prey to his lustful desire. In lust, he took another man's wife. Her name was Bathsheba. Theirs was a shameful, murderous affair in that David arranged for Bathsheba's husband, Uriah, to be killed in battle.

The consequences were immense. David's son, born to Bathsheba, died shortly after birth. In addition, his home fell apart . . . the famous shepherd-king endured years of heartache and embarrassment at the hands of his rebellious children. He bore such long and agonizing consequences because of one night's foolish passion.

But David didn't die in prison. Instead, he died a man of honor and dignity . . . the anointed king of Israel . . . "a man after God's own heart." What made the difference?

Repentance.

In brokenness and humility David called on the Lord for forgiveness and found mercy and grace to go on. Let me ask you a series of questions.

- Are you dancing on the edge of disaster today?
- Are you living a secret life that only you and God know about?
- Have you allowed yourself to become so addicted to your sin that you fear there's no possibility of turning back?

You need to know that it's never too late to start doing what's right. You cannot sink so deep in sin that Christ is unable to lift you from despair. Repentance is the place to start. That means you turn from your sin and confess to Him your failure to obey and your inability to change on your own. Ask for His strength to overcome. Stop rationalizing what you're doing. You're only fooling yourself. You may have kept it secret so far . . . but ultimately you will be found out. Don't go another day without falling on your knees before God and praying with David,

Be gracious to me, O God, according to Your lovingkindess;
According to the greatness of Your compassion blot out my
   transgressions.
Wash me thoroughly from my iniquity
And cleanse me from my sin.
For I know my transgressions,
And my sin is ever before me.
Against You, You only, I have sinned
And done what is evil in Your sight,
So that you are justified when You speak
And blameless when You judge . . .
   . . . Create in me a clean heart, O God,
And renew a steadfast spirit within me.
Do not cast me away from Your presence
And do not take Your Holy Spirit from me. Restore to me the
   joy of Your salvation
And sustain me with a willing spirit. (Psalm 51:1–4, 10–12)

Did you pray that prayer . . . *honestly* and *sincerely*? Now you need to reconnect with a fellow Christian who can help you fully recover. Confess your sin. Ask for help. If necessary, seek out a qualified Christian counselor who can assist you in your full recovery.

And then? Get back in the race . . . and run like you've never run before!

Fourteen

Getting Through the Tough Stuff of Death

THE LATE AUTHOR Joseph Bayly knew a lot about death. He had experienced its sting too many times. His newborn son died after surgery, his five-year-old boy died from leukemia, and his eighteen-year-old was killed in a sledding accident complicated by mild hemophilia. Each encounter taught him a different lesson on the painful reality of death. He writes truthfully and soberly about the subject in the opening of his book *The Last Thing We Talk About.*

> The hearse began its grievous journey many thousand years ago, as a litter made of saplings.
>
> Litter, sled, wagon, Cadillac: the conveyance has changed, but the corpse it carries is the same.
>
> Birth and death enclose a man in a sort of parenthesis of the present. And the brackets at the beginning and end of life are still impenetrable.

This frustrates us, especially in a time of scientific break-through and exploding knowledge, that we should be able to break out of earth's environment and yet be stopped cold by death's unyielding mystery. Electroencephalogram may replace mirror held before the mouth, autopsies may become more sophisticated, cosmetic embalming may take the place of pennies on the eyelids and canvas shrouds, but death continues to confront us with its blank wall. Everything changes; death is changeless. . . .

Dairy farmer and sales executive live in death's shadow, with Nobel Prize winner and prostitute, mother, infant, teen, old man. The hearse stands waiting for the surgeon who transplants a heart as well as the hopeful recipient, for the funeral director as well as the corpse he manipulates.

Death spares none.[1]

What powerful, penetrating words written by one who had become all too familiar with death. Yet it's that intensity of reflection we must all embrace if we are to get through the tough stuff of death during our days on earth. It will take that kind of honesty. Still, very few people willingly face their mortality, let alone talk openly about it. It is worth our time to consider some of the more common ways people deal with the reality of death.

FAMILIAR REACTIONS TO THE SUBJECT OF DEATH

Many people choose humor. A bumper sticker I saw several years ago said it all:

Don't take life so seriously!
You won't get out of it alive anyway.

You're likely smiling right now. Made me chuckle too. Frequently that's how many people handle death—by keeping the subject light and humorous. Somehow making a joke out of it keeps death at a safe distance. We never have to face the reality of it.

If you were to take a couple of months and record each time you hear a joke about death, you'd be amazed at the large number. Talk-show comedians make light of the subject and so do cartoonists. Woody Allen once quipped, "It's not that I'm afraid to die. I just don't want to be there when it happens."

One humorous story I enjoyed recently told of a couple who had been married for more than fifty years, but whose marriage had been rather stormy. Eventually the husband died, and it fell to the wife to choose a grave marker. She contacted a stonecutter to relay her choice of stone to be used. She said over the phone, "Look, I don't want to be fancy. I certainly don't wish to spend a lot of money. But I do think I ought to have a stone there, marking my husband's grave. Let's keep it brief and simple. Why don't you just engrave the words, 'To My Husband,' in a suitable place on the stone?" He said, "That'll be fine. I'll take care of it."

He finished cutting the marker and engraving the words before calling the woman to come and see it at the cemetery. She arrived prepared to see a clean-cut grave marker with the words, "To My Husband," engraved in a suitable place. Instead, to her horror she saw,

To My Husband . . . In a Suitable Place

For many folks a humorous story helps mask the pain and confusion surrounding death. So a common reaction to death is to keep it funny.

Another familiar reaction is denial. Don't talk about death—just remove it from all conversation and reflection. Pretend it doesn't exist. It's easier for folks not to talk about death's reality than to wrestle with its meaning.

I recall as a boy riding along with my parents in the car and seeing a dead animal on the side of the road. I hated seeing those little critters lying lifeless on the pavement. It made me think of my own pets. When I'd groan or whimper, my mother would simply say, "Just don't look at it, honey. Just look away." From our early years you and I were encouraged to look the other way—to put death out of our minds. It's why we purchase life insurance instead of death insurance. Let's face it . . . who wants to buy death coverage? Life is a much easier sell!

Again, Joe Bayly writes,

> We are critical of the Victorians because they sentimentalized death and surrounded it with pathos. But modern man denies it. The sort of taboo Victorians placed on public discussion of sex has been transferred to death in our culture. . . .
>
> This conspiracy of silence . . . has produced a denial of death without precedent in Western civilization. [2]

Others choose to romanticize death by relying on elaborate flower arrangements and graceful hymns to emphasize death's supposed beauty. There's certainly nothing wrong with beautiful tributes honoring our loved ones who have died. Yet it's all designed to bring a brighter, more meaningful element to those painful, final good-byes.

One more time, Bayly notes,

> Coronary, cancer, stroke, infection. Death comes, even normally, in a multitude of ways, to every human condition, every age.

Shall we deny death and try to make it beautiful?

A corpse is never beautiful, animal corpse or corpse of man. . . .

We cannot beautify death. We may live with it and accept it,

but we cannot change its foul nature.[3]

I think Bayly is right. In spite of all our human attempts to veil death's horror, we cannot escape it. Death is our final enemy and represents the door through which we all must pass from this life to the next.

The final reaction to death is fear. People fear death like few other realities.

I recall an elderly woman years ago during a visit I made to her home. Her words, said through tears, are still fresh in my mind: "Pastor Chuck, I am so afraid to die." I told her that was the most natural feeling on earth. Fear accompanies our thoughts of death.

Fear and death are constant companions. If you don't think people are afraid to die, observe how your fellow passengers on an airplane react when air turbulence causes sudden drops and shudders during a flight. I've heard people young and old shriek and cry out. Fear of death plagues the human soul.

Unfortunately sooner or later we will be forced to face death head-on. When you or a loved one lies dying, death will not be funny or distant or beautiful . . . and it need not be fearful. One thing it will be is *real.* Perhaps painfully real.

Mary and Martha, two very close friends of Jesus, understood the reality of death. They became caught in its painful and inescapable web when their brother, Lazarus, was struck with a terminal illness. In this touching story recorded in John chapter 11, we witness the full range of human emotion on display. Best of all, we discover how Christ helped get them through the tough stuff of death.

A POIGNANT STORY OF GRIEF AND DEATH

There was no laughter in the ancient hamlet of Bethany. Fear, anger, and doubt had stolen whatever semblance of stability and peace that had once been there. Certainly no beauty was found there either. Instead, an ominous cloud of uncertainty hung heavy over the home where Lazarus lay dying. John writes, "Now a certain man was sick, Lazarus of Bethany, the village of Mary and her sister Martha" (John 11:1). Lazarus was a trusted friend of Jesus, the bachelor brother of Martha and Mary, his two older sisters. Without warning, Lazarus had fallen into a serious illness. His fever rose as the sickness refused to leave. Perhaps the doctors came and left shaking their heads in bewilderment. If there was such, the medicine didn't help either. Repeated attempts at curing the illness ended unsuccessfully. When Lazarus's condition grew more grim, John tells us, "The sisters sent word to Him, saying, 'Lord, behold he whom You love is sick'" (v. 3).

Close friends don't need an invitation to come to the bedside of a dying loved one. Mary and Martha quickly informed Jesus of their brother's serious condition, knowing that if anyone could help it would be the Master. Surely He would drop everything and get to Bethany without hesitation. Lazarus's condition worsened.

Sickness Turns to Death

Strangely, yet deliberately, Jesus chose not to go to Bethany right away. He didn't even go the next day . . . or the next. He still tarried. As the sisters had feared, Lazarus died. He was gone. He lay there with no pulse. No brain waves. A lifeless corpse. I repeat, it wasn't funny, unreal, or beautiful. It was not only real; it was Martha and Mary's worst nightmare. And on top of the loss of their brother came great feelings of anger his sisters felt toward Jesus for delaying

His coming. Their disillusionment knew no bounds. They had grown desperate, expecting Jesus to arrive in time to heal their brother before the disease took its final toll. But He never showed up. We can only imagine the heartache mixed with hostility Mary and Martha felt toward Jesus, in fact, toward their God. Faith is put to the maximum test when death crushes the hope of healing.

The Blame Game

News of Lazarus's death finally reached Jesus. Back in Bethany, friends come from all over the region to grieve with Mary and Martha (John 11:17–19). In the meantime Jesus finally decides to come alongside His friends. On His arrival, Martha meets Him on the road, leaving Mary at the house to grieve. Martha looked Jesus square in the eye and said, "Lord, if You had been here, my brother would not have died" (v. 21). Her accusing tone is eloquent and forceful. She felt betrayed, let down, and grossly disappointed in the only One who could have saved her brother's life. Where was He?

This scene was reenacted centuries later at the Grand Canyon, after a tragic midair collision. More than one hundred people died. Grimly, most of the body parts were strewn across the vast canyon. It was a ghastly scene. As best they could, rescuers gathered the scattered remains of the victims. The unenviable task of presiding over the memorial service fell to a young local minister. He knew virtually no one who had perished. Trembling and unsure of himself, he spoke of the faithfulness and goodness of God as he extolled His sovereign presence over all things. One grieving man grew indignant at the young pastor's words. Unable to remain silent, he burst forth in a loud voice and yelled, "If God is so good, and if He cares so much, then where was He when *this* happened?"

Thousands asked and are still asking that searching question in the aftermath of September 11, 2001—that horrible, surreal day when more than three thousand innocent people died in the series of violent terrorist attacks on our country. Where *was* God on September 11, 2001? We should have no difficulty understanding Martha's struggle. The tough stuff of death brings to the surface any number of raw, unguarded emotions.

Martha was flat-out angry. She couldn't believe Jesus had waited so long. She questioned His compassion. She doubted His goodness.

Maybe you're questioning the Lord these days. Perhaps you're lost in a fog of fear and confusion as you process what it means to live out your days alone, without the comfort and companionship of your mate. Maybe you're wondering why God would let your teenage son get into that car with his drunken friend at the wheel. Where was God when your beautiful young daughter walked out of her apartment on her way to work and vanished in the black night? Where was God when searchers stumbled upon her broken body, decaying in a field? Why didn't God heal your wife *before* the cancer reached her brain? How come God didn't stop your son's military patrol vehicle from driving into an enemy ambush? Why was your baby born with that inoperable condition that took her life while she was so young, so innocent? Why, why, why, why, why?

Could Jesus have saved Lazarus from death? Absolutely. Could He have prevented it? Of course. Amazingly, He didn't. He deliberately chose to wait. Lazarus's death was part of His sovereign, grander plan. His plan contradicts our preferences. There's a divine mystery in all of this. His ways are not our ways.

There will come a day when God will deliberately allow death to have its way in your life and mine. You and I will one day succumb to death's stranglehold. We, too, will die. Our loved ones will all eventually die. For some it will be before the end of this year. For many it will be before the end of this decade. For some it will seem terribly premature. For a few it will be accidental, even tragic. Some may die horribly, as the victims of terrorist attacks. We know neither the time nor the manner in which we will breathe our last. Nevertheless death remains certain for all.

Someday in the future, when you and I least expect it, our number will come up. When that occurs, it is possible that our loved ones will question God. They will wonder why God chose not to intervene. "Why didn't You bring healing?" they may ask. As in those dark days in Bethany, grief will sweep over our loved ones as they are forced to face exactly what Martha and Mary endured . . . the final tolling of the bells.

But was it final?

A Miraculous Prayer

As Jesus approached the place where Lazarus had been buried, some of the people in the crowd began to accuse Jesus. John recalls, "Some of them said, 'Could not this man, who opened the eyes of the blind man, have kept this man also from dying?'" (v. 37). Doubt intensified in the minds of the grieving, especially among those whose faith rested on unsure footing. Overwhelmed by their unbelief and sadness, Jesus said simply, "Remove the stone" (v. 39).

Remove the stone? Surely He was not serious. Opening a closed grave was downright unorthodox and seems cruel to some. What did He mean, *remove the stone?* Such audacity! Martha and the others protested loudly. Their disbelief is on display in her words: "Lord, by this time there will be a stench, for he has been dead four days" (v. 39). His request made no sense to Martha. It seemed to her both unkind and distasteful. Jesus's response is worth noting:

> "Did I not say to you that if you believe, you will see the glory of God?" So they removed the stone. Then Jesus raised His eyes, and said, "Father, I thank You that You have heard Me. I knew that You always hear Me; but because of the people standing around I said it, so that they may believe that You sent Me." When He had said these things, He cried out with a loud voice, "Lazarus, come forth." (John 10:40–43)

To this day in Israel there are gravesites carved into hillsides. Sometimes the soft limestone is cut away, lots of dirt and rock removed, and a body is placed in the hollowed-out tomb. A large stone is then used to close off the opening of the shallow cave and protect the remains from animals and even grave robbers. The final part of the grieving process occurs when that large circular-shaped stone is rolled into place. Jesus commanded the stone across Lazarus's grave to be removed. He then issued another command: "Lazarus, come forth!" (v. 43).

From Fear to Faith

An eerie hush enveloped the crowd. Everyone frowned and stared in silence. What in the world was Jesus up to, calling Lazarus to come out of the tomb? Please understand, if Lazarus had *resurrected,* there would have been no reason to remove the stone. A resurrected body would have had the ability to come *through* the stone. Lazarus would have had a glorified body, able to pass from one place to the next, unhindered by matter and space (20:19–20). Jesus had the stone removed; so Lazarus, having been *resuscitated* from death, could walk out alive.

Mary and Martha stood frozen in disbelief. Suddenly they saw something move within the shadowy darkness of the tomb. Could it be? Was it true? Lazarus—alive? Yes, he was alive . . . miraculously brought back from beyond after having died four days before!

John writes simply, "The man who had died came forth, bound hand and foot with wrappings, and his face was wrapped around with a cloth. Jesus said to them, 'Unbind him, and let Him go'" (11:44).

Jesus viewed the gravesite as a place from which new life would spring. First, new life would emerge from Lazarus's lifeless body. Second, new life within would begin in those who had been spiritually dead in their sin.

I've observed throughout my ministry that death causes even the most careless of souls to pause long enough to ponder eternal things. That is exactly the case with Lazarus's death. John tells us, "Many of the Jews who came to Mary, and saw what He had done, believed in Him" (v. 45). What they witnessed changed their hearts. It still happens. When Jesus meets us in the tough stuff of death, we can be made alive through His resurrection power.

That's why we must instill in others not only the reality of death but, even more importantly, the hope of eternal life—Jesus's promise of resurrection. This life is only a fleeting prelude to eternal life to come. How valuable it is to live our lives knowing that every new day is a gift, every new year a treasure. What Mary, Martha, and those nameless people who made up that somber crowd witnessed was a magnificent, life-transforming miracle. No doubt, from that point on, each viewed life with a keener appreciation for its meaning and value.

A question comes to mind right now: How would you have felt being the person to unbind Lazarus and let him go? Think before answering. Try to imagine yourself unwrapping his body, then

217

standing back and seeing Lazarus, dead as stone only moments before, walk out into the bright sunlight.

What about You? Will You Believe?

Before we leave this remarkable story, let's rewind the tape to a place I intentionally waited to observe. Jesus mentions two promises He would fulfill by waiting to come to Bethany. He gave the first promise to Martha when she met Him, sobbing on the road. He said, "Your brother will rise again" (John 11:23). He promised Martha that she would see her brother alive again. He would not remain in the cold, dark tomb. He would experience the miracle of new life.

The second promise Jesus spoke to all who could hear. In fact, He *continues* to make it to all people everywhere.

And what is that second promise? Let me write it in a way you cannot misunderstand. Jesus said, "I am, right now, Resurrection and Life. The one who believes in me, even though he or she dies, will live. And everyone who lives believing in Me does not ultimately die at all. Do you believe this?" (vv. 25–26 MSG). That is the fundamental question of life. *Do you believe this?* That's the question you will need to ask in the middle of your grief. Each one of us must answer Christ's penetrating query: *Do you believe this?*

It turns out that the goofy bumper sticker I mentioned earlier was dead wrong: "Don't take life too seriously. You won't get out of it alive anyway!" Wrong! Quite the opposite is true. Take life *and* death seriously. You *do* get out of it alive. You will live forever . . . somewhere. We all face a life after death. The question is not, "Will I live forever?" but, "Where will I live forever?" After your death you will be resurrected (not resuscitated). Lazarus came back to life only to die again. When you come back, you will *live on*. The question, I repeat, is *where*?

Jesus alone has the power of resurrection. Our assurance of spending forever with Him depends on how we answer the question He asks Lazarus's sister, "Do you believe this?"

The One who performed that unforgettable miracle on Lazarus, later went to the cross, hung there, and died, paying the complete penalty for your sin and mine. His loved ones wrapped His body in burial cloths and placed Him in a grave; then they sealed His tomb with a stone. Three days later, He was alive! Gone from the grave! Resurrected to life—never to die again. Jesus conquered death and removed its sting forever.

Do you believe this?

Sometime after Jesus had left the earth, Saul of Tarsus did too. After he became the apostle Paul, he not only believed in the power of the Resurrection, he became so convinced of it, he wrote that neither "death, nor life, nor angels, nor principalities, nor things present, nor things to come, nor powers, nor height, nor depth, nor any other created thing, will be able to separate us from the love of God, which is in Christ Jesus our Lord" (Romans 8:38–39).

That's why, toward the end of his magnificent life, Paul could say with confidence, "For me, to live is Christ, and to die is gain" (Philippians 1:21). He faced his own death without fear because of His relationship with Christ. And what a relationship it was!

In light of that, I want to close this chapter with an extended, almost poetic excerpt from John Pollock's splendid work *The Apostle: A Life of Paul.* If you're facing the tough stuff of death, or you're walking the extremely lonely and painful path of watching a loved one die, allow this author's moving words to sink into your soul. You will find comfort in his description of the great apostle, leaning hard on his Savior's promise—triumphantly facing the reality of his death. As you read these words, imagine having the courage to face your own death this courageously. It's possible, based on your faith in Christ alone.

The ancient tradition of Paul's execution site is almost certainly authentic but the details cannot be fixed. Whereas Christ's Via Dolorosa may be followed step by step, Paul's remains vague. He would have it so. And because Christ had walked that earlier road, Paul's was no Via Dolorosa, for they were walking it together: "Thanks be to God who in Christ always leads us in triumph." "For to me to live is Christ and to die is gain."

They marched him out through the walls past the pyramid of Cestius which still stands, on to the Ostian Way toward the sea. Crowds journeying to or from Ostia would recognize an execution squad by the lictors with their *fasces* of rods and axe, and the executioner carrying a sword, which in Nero's reign had replaced the ax; by the escort, and by the manacled criminal, walking stiffly and bandy-legged, ragged and filthy from his prison, but not ashamed or degraded. He was going to a feast, to a triumph, to the crowning day to which he had pressed forward. He who talked often of God's promise of eternal life in Jesus could not fear; he believed as he had spoken: "All God's promises find their 'yes' in Him." No executioner was going to lose him the conscious presence of Jesus; he was not changing his company, only the place where he enjoyed it. Better still, he would see Jesus. Those glimpses—on the Damascus road, in Jerusalem, at Corinth, on that sinking ship; now he was going to see him face to face, to know even as he had been known.

They marched Paul to the third milestone on the Ostian Way, to a little pinewood in a glade, probably a place of tombs, known then as Aquae Salviae or Healing Waters, and now as Tre Fontane where an abbey stands in his honor. He is believed to have been put overnight in a tiny cell, for this was a common place of execution. If Luke was allowed to stay by his window, if

Timothy or Mark had reached Rome in time, the sounds of night vigil would not be of weeping but singing: "as sorrowful yet always rejoicing; as dying and, behold, we live."

At first light, the soldiers took Paul to the pillar. The executioner stood ready, stark naked. Soldiers stripped Paul to the waist and tied him, kneeling upright, to the low pillar which left his neck free. Some accounts say the lictors beat him with rods; a beating had been the usual prelude to beheading but in recent years not always inflicted. If they must administer this last, senseless dose of pain to a body so soon to die, "Who shall separate us from the love of Christ? Shall tribulation . . . or sword?"

"I reckon that the sufferings of this present time are not worthy to be compared with"—the flash of a sword—"the glory."[5]

Christ in you . . . the hope of glory! *Glory.* That is what awaits the soul who has leaned on Jesus. Glory to God. Glory for you. Glory for me.

Please allow me to probe deeply into your soul. May I ask you, directly, what is going to get you beyond death into your eternal home? The answer is Christ. Only Christ. It is He alone who holds the promise of resurrection and the hope of life eternal. He conquered death for you and for me. You may be reading these closing words and fighting off tears of anguish and grief. Perhaps you just lost your mate of many years, or a child to a tragic accident, or a close friend to some dread disease. Christ understands your grief. Like no other, He feels your pain. He understands your despair. He's been there. He's felt those same feelings. He endured the same loneliness.

Or perhaps you sense that death is near for you. If you have never before trusted the Lord Jesus, then you must take care of that today. Don't wait for a more convenient time to call on His name. Believe on the Lord Jesus Christ, and you will be saved, meaning when you breathe your last, you will pass from death to life—life eternal.

If you know Christ, there is no reason to fear what lies beyond the grave. He's already there. He has prepared a place for you. It's ready. Unexplainable, unending joy will be yours forever, thanks to Jesus.

You can then exclaim with Paul, "'Death is swallowed up in victory. O Death, where is your victory? O Death, where is your sting?' The sting of death is sin, and the power of sin is the law; but thanks be to God who always gives us the victory through our Lord Jesus Christ!" (1 Corinthians 15:54).

And immediately following death—"the glory!"

Conclusion

It's Always Something!

I DON'T CARE HOW OLD YOU ARE, where you live, or what you do for a living; if you're single or married; childless or have a houseful of kids; own your home or rent your place . . . *it's always something.* It makes no difference which hobby you enjoy, who you know, how much money you make, whether you're a workaholic or completely retired from the workplace, whether you're a person who has little or no faith or you're a stronghearted follower of Jesus . . . *it's always something!*

Tough stuff happens in life and will continue to happen to you. Sometimes you and I bring it on ourselves. More often, however, we had nothing to do with why it occurred. There is simply no escape from the trials and the turmoil related to living on this planet. Only a quick glance at the past six months of your life is all it takes to convince you that this is true. Who would have ever guessed a year ago that you had all that in front of you? And your struggle, while it may differ in the details, has been duplicated in the life of every other individual around the globe.

One of my main reasons for writing this book was simply to come right out and say those things. Now that we've come to the end, I'm glad I did. I deliberately chose some of the more prominent areas that give us grief. We've covered temptation, misunderstanding, anxiety, and shame. We have also addressed the challenges of doubt, divorce, remarriage, confrontation, pain, and prejudice. And we didn't overlook those four giants everybody wrestles with: hypocrisy, inadequacy, disqualification, and death. There were several dozen other subjects I could have mentioned, but these are enough for now.

My hope, plain and simple, was first to come up front and say that nobody is immune from any of these things. And then I wanted to offer some hope that we can not only face them and come to terms with them but also get beyond them. Mainly I wanted to assure you that you are not alone in the struggle. The One who made you understands you. While He may push you to what seems to be your breaking point, He is never far away. Because He cares, He stays near, even though you can't see Him. And because He loves you, He will make sure you make it.

Not long ago I came across a story that illustrates this beautifully. It was told by an Episcopalian bishop from Colorado named William Frey and went something like this:

When I was an undergraduate at the University of Colorado in 1951, I spent a couple of hours a week reading to a fellow student. His name was John, and he was blind.

One day I asked him how he lost his sight. He told me of an accident that happened when he was a teenager and how, at that point, he had simply given up on life. "When the accident happened and I knew that I would never see again, I felt that life had ended, as far as I was concerned. I was bitter and angry with God for letting it happen, and I took my anger out on everyone around me. I felt that since I had no future, I wouldn't lift a finger on my own behalf. Let others wait on me. I shut my bedroom door and refused to come out except for meals."

The man I knew was an eager learner and an earnest student, so I had to ask what had changed his attitude. He told me this story. "One day, in exasperation, my father came into my room and started giving me a lecture. He said he was tired of my feeling sorry for myself. He said that winter was coming, and it was my job to put up the storm windows. 'You get those windows up by suppertime tonight, or else!' he shouted, slamming the door on his way out.

"Well," said John, "that made me so angry that I resolved to do it! Muttering and cursing to myself, I groped my way out to the garage, found the windows, a stepladder, all the necessary tools, and I went to work. *They'll be sorry when I fall off the ladder and break my neck,* I thought, but little by little, groping my way around the house, I got the job done."

Then he stopped, and his sightless eyes misted up as he told me, "I later discovered that at no time during the day had my father ever been more than four or five feet from my side."

The first assumption is that God is present—no more than an arm's length away—whether we're aware of it or not.[1]

Getting through the tough stuff is neither quick nor easy. It's what makes life seem harsh and unfair, sometimes even impossible. But knowing that we have our Father near can be just enough to keep us on our feet and able to take on whatever tomorrow may include. Since *it's always something* . . . the good news is this: *He's always there.*

Endnotes

INTRODUCTION
1. Charles B. Williams, *The New Testament in the Language of the People* (Nashville: Broadman and Holman Publishers, 1930; Montreat, NC: Sprawls Educational Publishing, 1999), 442. Used by permission.

CHAPTER I • *Getting Through the Tough Stuff of Temptation*
1. Robert Frost, "The Road Not Taken," in *The Poetry of Robert Frost*, ed. Edward Connery Lathem (New York: Henry Holt and Company, copyright © 1969), 105. Used by permission.
2. William Barclay, *The Gospel of Matthew*, rev. ed., (Louisville, KY: Westminster John Knox Press, 1975), 1:66. Used by permission.
3. Ibid., p. 69. Used by permission.
4. Chuck Colson, personal communication with Charles R. Swindoll. Used by permission.
5. Martin Luther, "A Mighty Fortress Is Our God," translated by Frederick H. Hedge; based on Psalm 46 from *The Celebration Hymnal* (Nashville: Word/Integrity, 1997), 151. Original source in public domain.

CHAPTER 2 • *Getting Through the Tough Stuff of Misunderstanding*
1. Ralph Waldo Emerson (1803-1882), "Essay II Self-Reliance," in *Essays,* (1841), corrected and republished as *Essays: First Series* (1847). Original source in public domain.
2. Archibald Thomas Robertson, *Word Pictures in the New Testament: The Gospel According to Matthew, The Gospel According to Mark* (Nashville: Broadman Press, 1930) 1:283. Used by permission.

CHAPTER 3 • *Getting Through the Tough Stuff of Anxiety*
1. "Top Ten Anxieties for the 1990s," published by the National Anxiety Center in Maplewood, NJ. Used by permission from Alan Caruba, founder.

2. John Trent, and Gary Smalley, *The Two Sides of Love* (Wheaton, IL: Tyndale House Publishers, 1990), 34–36. Used by permission.

3. Jeanne W. Hendricks, *A Woman for All Seasons* (Nashville: Thomas Nelson Publishers, 1977), 155–56. Used by permission of Jeanne W. Hendricks.

4. Catherine Marshall, ed., *The Prayers of Peter Marshall* (Grand Rapids: Chosen Books, a division of Baker Publishing Group, 1954), 36. Used by permission.

CHAPTER 4 • *Getting Through the Tough Stuff of Shame*

1. William Riley Wilson, *The Execution of Jesus: A Judicial, Literary and Historical Investigation* (New York: Simon & Schuster, 1970), 152.

2. Bernard of Clairvaux, "O Sacred Head, Now Wounded" (Nashville: Word Music/Integrity Music, 1997), 316. Original source in public domain.

3. William Barclay, *The Gospel of John,* rev. ed. (Louisville, KY: Westminster John Knox Press, 1975), 2:1–2. Used by permission.

4. Catherine Marshall, *A Man Called Peter: The Story of Peter Marshall* (Grand Rapids: Chosen Books, a division of Baker Publishing Group, 1949), 314. Used by permission.

5. John Bunyan, *Pilgrim's Progress* (Uhrichsville, OH: Barbour Books, an imprint of Barbour Publishing), 36. Used by permission.

CHAPTER 5 • *Getting Through the Tough Stuff of Doubt*

1. Edward M. Plass, comp., *What Luther Says: An Anthology,* (St. Louis: Concordia Publishing House, 1972), 426. Original source in public domain.

2. Alfred Tennyson, "In Memoriam," in *Baker's Pocket Treasury of Religious Verse,* Donald T. Kauffman, comp. (Grand Rapids: Baker Book House, 1962), 174. Used by permission.

3. Daniel Talor, *The Myth of Certainty* (Downers Grove, IL: InterVarsity Press, subsidiary rights owned by Daniel Taylor, 1986), 14–15. Used by permission.

4. Ibid., 16. Used by permission.

5. Merrill C. Tenney, *John: The Gospel of Belief, An Analytic Study of the Text* (Grand Rapids: Wm. B. Eerdmans, 1948), 173. Used by permission. All rights reserved.

CHAPTER 6 • *Getting Through the Tough Stuff of Divorce*

1. Charles Haddon Spurgeon, *Lectures to My Students* (Grand Rapids: Zondervan, 1970), 70. Used by permission of The Zondervan Corporation.

2. John Powell, *Happiness is An Inside Job* (Allen, TX: RCL Enterprises Inc., 1989), 2-3. Used by permission.

3. John R. W. Stott, *The Message of the Sermon on the Mount (Matthew 5–7): Christian Counter-Culture* (Downers Grove, IL: InterVarsity Press, 1978), 95. Used by permission.

4. D. A. Carson, "Matthew" in *The Expositor's Bible Commentary* (Grand Rapids, MI: Regency Reference Library, Zondervan, 1984), 8:411. Used by permission of The Zondervan Corporation.

CHAPTER 7 • *Getting Through the Tough Stuff of Remarriage*
1. Mike Mason, *The Mystery of Marriage: As Iron Sharpens Iron* (Portland, OR: Multnomah, 1985), 74. Used by permission.
2. R. C. H. Lenski, *The Interpretation of St. Paul's First and Second Epistles to the Corinthians* (Peabody, MA: Hendrickson Publishers, 1937), 295. Public domain.

CHAPTER 8 • *Getting Through the Tough Stuff of Confrontation*
1. Gregory Titelman, *Random House Dictionary of America's Popular Proverbs and Sayings*, 2nd ed. (New York: Random House Reference, Random House, 2000), 89. Used by permission.
2. Based on the outlines and transcripts of the sermons of Charles R. Swindoll and coauthored by Lee Hough, *Christ at the Crossroads Bible Study Guide* (Plano, TX: Insight for Living, 1998), 91. Used by permission.
3. William Barclay, *The Gospel of Matthew* (Louisville, KY: Westminster John Knox Press, 1957), 2:163. Used by permission.
4. David Augsberger, *Caring Enough to Confront* (Ventura, CA: Gospel Light/Regal Books, 1973), 13. Used by permission.

CHAPTER 9 • *Getting Through the Tough Stuff of Pain*
1. Webster's New Collegiate Dictionary, s.v. "pain."
2. Philip Yancey, *Where Is God When It Hurts* (Grand Rapids: Zondervan, 1977, 1990), 22–23. Used by permission of The Zondervan Corporation.
3. C. S. Lewis, *The Problem of Pain* (New York: Collier Books, Macmillan Publishing Company, 1962), 156. Copyright (c) C. S. Lewis Pte. Ltd. 1940. Extract reprinted by permission.
4. Philip P. Bliss, "Hallelujah, What a Savior!" Public Domain.

CHAPTER 10 • *Getting Through the Tough Stuff of Prejudice*
1. Excerpt from John Howard Griffin, *Black Like Me*, 2nd ed. Copyright (c) 1960, 1961, 1977 by John Howard Griffin. Reprinted by permission of Houghton Mifflin Company. All rights reserved.
2. Ibid., preface. Reprinted by permission of Houghton Mifflin Company. All rights reserved.
3. William James, quoted in *Bartlett's Familiar Quotations*, 16th ed. (Boston: Little, Brown and Co., 1991), 546. Original source in public domain.

ENDNOTES

CHAPTER II • *Getting Through the Tough Stuff of Hypocrisy*
1. Thomas R. Ybarra, quoted in Laurence J. Peter, *Peter's Quotation Ideas for Our Time* (New York: Harper Collins/William Morrow and Company, 1977), 84. Original source, "The Christian," (1909) in the public domain.
2. William Barclay, *The Gospel of Matthew,* rev. ed. (Louisville, KY: Westminster John Knox Press, rev. 1975), 1:197. Used by permission.
3. Ibid., 237. Used by permission.
4. Alfred Edersheim, *The Life and Times of Jesus the Messiah,* quoted in William Barclay, *The Gospel of Matthew,* rev. ed. (Louisville, KY: Westminster John Knox Press, 1975), 2:114. Used by permission.

CHAPTER 12 • *Getting Through the Tough Stuff of Inadequacy*
1. A. B. Bruce, *The Training of the Twelve* (Grand Rapids: Kregel Publications, 1971), 536-537. Public domain.

CHAPTER 13 • *Getting Through the Tough Stuff of Disqualification*
1. A. W. Tozer, *God Tells the Man Who Cares* (Harrisburg, PA: Christian Publications, 1970), 76. Used by permission.
2. William Barclay, *The Letters to the Corinthians* (Louisville, KY: Westminster John Knox Press, 1975), 85. Used by permission.
3. Henry Alford, *The Greek Testament: The Acts of the Apostle, The Epistles to the Romans and Corinthians,* 6th ed. (Boston: Lee, Shepard, and Dillingham, 1873), 2:551. Public domain.
4. Charles Haddon Spurgeon, *The Metropolitan Tabernacle Pulpit, Sermons Preached by C. H. Spurgeon.* Revised and Published during the Year 1908 (Pasadena, TX: Pilgrim Publications, 1978), 54:14–15. Public domain.

CHAPTER 14 • *Getting Through the Tough Stuff of Death*
1. Joseph Bayly, *The Last Thing We Talk About* (Elgin, IL: David C. Cook, a division of Cook Communications, 1982), 11–12. Dr. Swindoll would like to thank Mary Lou Bayly for permission to use excerpts from her late husband, Joe Bayly's book, *The Last Thing We Talk About,* currently published by Victor Books under the title, *A Voice in the Wilderness: The Best of Joe Bayly.*
2. Woody Allen, quoted on www.memorablequotations.com/woody.htm
3. Joseph Bayly, *The Last Thing We Talk About* (Elgin, IL: David C. Cook, a division of Cook Communications, 1982), 18.
4. Ibid., p. 15.
5. John Pollock, *The Man Who Shook the World* (Colorado Springs: Cook Communications, 1972, 1974. By arrangement with Doubleday & Company, Garden City, NY, publishers of the hardcover edition titled *The Apostle: A Life of Paul*), 237–38.

Endnotes

CONCLUSION • *It's Always Something!*
   1. William Frey, *The Dance of Hope* (Colorado Springs: WaterBrook Press, 2003), 174. Used by permission of WaterBrook Press. All rights reserved.

The Great Lives Series

In his Great Lives from God's Word Series, Charles Swindoll shows us how the great heroes of the faith offer a model of courage, hope, and triumph in the face of adversity.

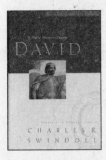

DAVID
A Man of
Passion and
Destiny

ESTHER
A Woman of
Strength and
Dignity

JOSEPH
A Man of
Integrity and
Forgiveness

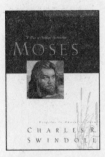

MOSES
A Man of
Selfless
Dedication

ELIJAH
A Man Who
Stood With
God

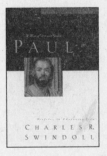

PAUL
A Man of
Grace and Grit

JOB
A Man of
Heroic
Endurance

W PUBLISHING GROUP™
www.wpublishinggroup.com